MICHAEL GAISMAIR

Revolutionary and Reformer

STUDIES
IN MEDIEVAL AND
REFORMATION THOUGHT

EDITED BY

HEIKO A. OBERMAN, Tübingen

IN COOPERATION WITH

E. JANE DEMPSEY DOUGLASS, Claremont, California
LEIF GRANE, Copenhagen
GUILLAUME H. M. POSTHUMUS MEYJES, Leiden
ANTON G. WEILER, Nijmegen

VOLUME XXIII

WALTER KLAASSEN

MICHAEL GAISMAIR
Revolutionary and Reformer

LEIDEN
E. J. BRILL
1978

MICHAEL GAISMAIR

Revolutionary and Reformer

BY

WALTER KLAASSEN

LEIDEN
E. J. BRILL
1978

This book has been published with the help of a grant from the Humanities Research Council of Canada, using funds provided by the Canada Council.

ISBN 90 04 05673 4

PRINTED IN THE NETHERLANDS

TABLE OF CONTENTS

PREFACE

The years 1974 to 1976 were unusually rich in new research into and interpretations of the Peasant Revolt of 1524-1526. This little volume is a contribution to that research. The story of Michael Gaismair has already been expertly told by Josef Macek, notable Czech historian, in his book *Der Tiroler Bauernkrieg und Michael Gaismair*. But that work is inaccessible to most English-speaking students of the Peasant Revolt. Besides, it does not seriously concern itself with the external influences and the inner process that made a revolutionary and a reformer of Gaismair.

I have attempted to fill this lacuna. I have shown that Gaismair was a man of his time and not a modern secularist as Macek occasionally implies. Moreover, I have been able to add to and correct Macek's work at a number of points in terms of historical details.

I owe special thanks to Dr. George H. Williams of Harvard University for first directing my attention to Gaismair. The sabbatical leave policy of Conrad Grebel College enabled me to do the basic research and writing during the years 1970-1971.

I acknowledge my indebtedness to the people working in the various archives in which I was privileged to work; to Hofrat Dr. Hanns Bachmann and his staff, as well as to his successor Hofrat Dr. Eduard Widmoser of the Tiroler Landesarchiv in Innsbruck for the many hours of friendly and prompt service; to the late Dr. Otto Kostenzer of the library of the Landesmuseum Ferdinandeum in Innsbruck for directing me to materials so far unknown to Gaismair research; to Canon Dr. Karl Wolfsgruber for helping me with archivalia and sage advice at the Archivio vescovile Bressanone (Brixen), Italy; to Dr. A. Casetti of the L'archivio di Stato Bolzano in Bolzano (Bozen) and his staff for their willing assistance; to staff in the Staatsarchiv and the Stadtarchiv in Zürich for helping me clear up some doubtful matters.

My appreciation goes to Mrs. Pauline Bauman who carefully typed the manuscript twice, as well as to a reader whose name I do not know for vigorous but always constructive criticism. Most of his suggestions for improvement were accepted, thus making a much better product. I am grateful to the Humanities Research Council of Canada for making a generous grant which made possible the publication of the book.

Finally, according to a well-established but laudable custom, I take a bow to my wife Ruth. Upon a snowy evening on the Innrain in Innsbruck I was sharing with her some of the findings of my research on Gaismair which I was planning to publish in the form of several articles. She first spied a book at the end of my research, and has given her ready encouragement and advice toward its completion.

Conrad Grebel College
University of Waterloo,
Waterloo, Ontario
May Day, 1977   WALTER KLAASSEN

ABBREVIATIONS OF PRIMARY AND SECONDARY SOURCES CITED

AKM	*An die Königliche Majestät*
AFD	*An die fürstliche Durchlaucht*
AGAT	*Archiv für Geschichte und Altertumskunde Tirols*
ASB	*L'archivio di Stato Bolzano*
AVB	*Archivio vescovile Bressanone*
CD	*Causa Domini*
HR	*Hofregistratur* IV 30 A 106 and 105
JGGPÖ	*Jahrbuch der Gesellschaft für die Geschichte des Protestantismus in Österreich*
Macek I	*Der Tiroler Bauernkrieg und Michael Gaismair*
Macek II	"Zu den Anfängen des Tiroler Bauernkrieges. Der Landtag der Bauern in Meran und die Meraner Artikel", *Historica* I Prague, 1959
Macek III	"Das revolutionäre Programm des deutschen Bauernkrieges von 1526", *Historica* II, Prague, 1960
RN	*Registrum Notularum Sebastiani Sprenz Episcopi Brixinen De Annis 1521-1525. Codex X*
TE	*Tiroler Empörung.* Codex no. 1974
TGQ	*Tiroler Geschichtsquellen III*
TLRA	*Tiroler Landesregierungsarchiv*
VKM	*Von der Königlichen Majestät*
ZSW	*Zwingli: Sämtliche Werke*

CHAPTER ONE

THE REVOLT IN TYROL IN 1525 AND MICHAEL GAISMAIR

In the year 1549 mayor and council of the city of Zürich officially interceded with the government in Innsbruck for Michael Gaismair, junior. They requested that he be allowed to inherit some of his late father's estate which had been confiscated by the Innsbruck authorities because, as the intercession stated, "he had changed his religion". To this the Innsbruck officials replied [1] that if their "wise, cherished, and good friends" in Zürich had known the truth they would never have made the intercession. His property was confiscated not simply because he had changed his religion. The letter continues to outline the true reason:

> In order that you may have exact knowledge of the matter, and in order that you will excuse us for not being able to aid you in your request, we now share with you the true state of affairs: Michael Gaismair senior was the chief agitator, ringleader, and commander in the recent peasant rebellion against his Roman and royal majesty, our most gracious Lord, his sovereign (*Landesfürst*), and against all the authorities and the honourable estates [2] of Tyrol. He forgot his oath and promise and thus perjured himself and became faithless. When his wicked rebellious plan failed he was still not satisfied, but attempted to invade and injure this royal domain of Tyrol with a rebellious force.... He would have left nothing undone that might have contributed to the destruction of all authority and the honourable estates. [2]

---

[1] Printed in Karl Schadelbauer, "Drei Schreiben über Michael Gaismair im Staatsarchiv zu Zürich", *Tiroler Heimat* N.F. III, 1930, 98. Writer's translation.
Damit wir aber der Sachen grundtliche wissen empfahen und uns, das wir euch in eurem begeren mit willfaren, entschuldigt haben mugt, hat es diese gestalt :der alt Michel Gaismair ist in verschiner pewrischer empörung der obrist aufwigler, rädlfuerer und haubtman der pewrischen empörung wider die Rö. Kn. M. unsers allergnedigisten herrn also seinen landsfursten und alle andere ober und erberkhait in Tirol gewesen, seins aids und glubds vergessen und also an seinen landsfursten mainaidig und treulos worden, sich an demselben nit ersettigt sonder darnach als im sein pös aufruerisch vorhaben nit fort gen wellen, sich understanden diese furstliche grafschaft Tirol mit ainem aufruerigen volkh zu uber ziehen und zu beschedigen, auch an ainem ort dardurch gezogen und sovil an ime gewesen nichts underlassen, des zu vertilgung aller ober und erberkhait ime het furstendig sein mugen, und ain offner feind seins aigen vaterlands worden und also erstorben, dadurch er das hoch laster belaidigter maiestat begangen . . .
[2] A comprehensive term denoting the well-to-do propertied citizens.

...Thus he became a public enemy of his own fatherland and died in that state. He committed the major crime of lèse majesté.

That evaluation of Michael Gaismair, the leader of the Peasants' Revolt in Tyrol, became the standard justification of Tyrolians for trying to hide this "skeleton" in the proverbial family closet. As a man acting in a national crisis he was certainly superior in his abilities to Andreas Hofer, the much celebrated and legendary Tyrolian hero of 1809. A powerful man with a wide range of skills, of uncommon intelligence, and of a simple directness and sincerity, he had none of the intemperateness that characterized his revolutionary contemporary Thomas Müntzer. Rather he is revealed as a steady, reliable man, completely uncorrupted by his secretarial profession which was proverbial for bureaucratic arrogance and ruthlessness. He was a very capable organizer and administrator and an outstanding military leader. He had a firm grasp of all the problems facing his people and was especially expert in legal matters. More than that, he had a comprehensive grasp of events and movements and power alignments far beyond his native Tyrol, and developed considerable diplomatic skill which he exercised on the European stage.

In fact, what most distinguished Gaismair from other contemporary peasant leaders was the international character of his activity. His passionate commitment to the cause of the peasants in his homeland made of him a European figure. He was forced into involuntary exile by the Habsburg vendetta against him, a fact that would have ended the revolutionary activity of a lesser man. Gaismair continued the fight from foreign bases. He found asylum in Zürich, gathered an international army of peasants in the Grisons and Appenzell, fought with them in Salzburg, and finally took them to the Republic of Venice to continue the resistance from there.

Repeatedly he was involved in the construction of anti-Habsburg alliances involving Zürich, the south German free cities, and Venice. Several times he laid specific plans to invade Tyrol with the help of Zürich, an alliance based on religious sympathies. For six years he was allied with the Venetian Republic serving with high military distinction in return for aid to further his own revolutionary plans. His invasion of Tyrol in 1526 was undertaken because of his conviction that the League of Cognac, the anti-Habsburg coalition of France, Venice, and the Papacy, would simultaneously attack Tyrol from the south.

The fact that his European diplomacy was unsuccessful and that he repeatedly miscalculated in his expectations of foreign help does nothing to diminish the international stature of the erstwhile secretary. He was a man to be reckoned with. Evidence for this is the word of the French ambassador to Venice in 1526 that the French King did not wish to support Gaismair so that he could start another peasant war in Germany. He was unquestionably the most influential Tyrolian of his time.

However, unlike Gaismair, Andreas Hofer turned his talents against a foreign enemy, a fact which still brings him reverence and adulation. Gaismair opposed the enemy within the gates, the repressive powers of a waning feudal establishment, the Habsburg monarchy, and a corrupt church, and this has been his fatal disability. His countrymen have never forgiven him for his resistance to sovereign and church even though his name is immortalized in street names in Innsbruck and Bolzano.

A combination of factors conspired to keep this remarkable man and the revolt he led practically unknown until recently. To begin with, the Tyrolian revolt was part of the large conflagration of 1524-1525 in the German-speaking lands which is customarily discussed as part of the Lutheran reformation. Since during those years the Reformation had hardly spread beyond the borders of Germany, and since most of the action took place there, the Tyrolian part of the peasant uprising tends to be regarded as unimportant. Short treatments in general histories cannot deal with it, and general treatments like those of Günther Franz [3] and even of Engels understandably give it only proportionally scant attention. He was a more important and able peasant leader than Müntzer, but he did not have the "advantage" of being an antagonist of Luther as Müntzer did.

But the major reason for Gaismair's obscurity has already been alluded to above. Gaismair has been a *Schreckgespenst* for his own countrymen, as though the seven-year nightmare which he was to Ferdinand I had gone into the castle of Tyrolian consciousness to haunt it through the centuries. He does not even share the happy lot of Guy Fawkes, who at least lives on as a kind of antihero in legend and children's rhymes. An historiographical survey of the extant Tyrolian literature, added to this work as an appendix, will further illustrate what has been said.

---

[3] Günther Franz, *Der Deutsche Bauernkrieg*, Darmstadt Wissenschaftliche Buchgesellschaft, 1972, 157-164, 172-173; Friedrich Engels, *Der Deutsche Bauernkrieg*, Dietz Verlag, Berlin, 1965, 130-133.

The main purpose of this work is to fill the gaps in the story of Gaismair's thought heretofore left unattended to. Even Josef Macek in his monumental *Der Tiroler Bauernkrieg und Michael Gaismair* did not analyze either the letters or the Constitution of Gaismair in detail in the context of the course of Gaismair's life as a revolutionary leader and of the influences that played on him. No one had noticed the basically biblical orientation of the Constitution. Such recognition makes Macek's claim to Gaismair's basic secularity untenable. The analysis of the Constitution shows it to be, as had been said repeatedly by others, a completely unique political document. But its thoroughly biblical orientation further reveals a program for religious reform, also unique for its time.

The plan then is first to describe conditions in Tyrol at the time of the revolt, review Gaismair's biography and his evolution into a revolutionary, to tell again the story of the uprising and Gaismair's leadership, and then to analyze his brief writings and his reported words in the context of his activities for the shape of his thought.

The writings reveal a deeply religious man of strongly independent convictions. He was driven by a vision of social justice for his homeland which he found sketched out in the book of Deuteronomy. He had a profound sense of having been chosen by God to liberate his homeland from godless oppressors and to establish there a truly christian social order.

1. CONDITIONS IN TYROL 1525: CAUSES OF THE REVOLT

In some ways Tyrol was better off than the rest of Europe before the Peasants' Revolt broke out. The farmers were not as oppressed. In northern Tyrol farmers owned approximately one-third of the arable acreage.[4] Nor was the general oppression of the subjects by the overlords quite as severe as elsewhere.[5] The church had less landed property in Tyrol than in Germany and some limits were set to its exploitive practices.[6] Unlike the rest of Europe the farmers were represented in the Diet which gave them a means for resisting and reducing exploitation.[7] Serfdom was practically gone in Tyrol in 1525.[8] Finally, the country had a major source of wealth in its ex-

---

[4] J. Macek, *Der Tiroler Bauernkrieg und Michael Gaismair*, Deutscher Verlag der Wissenschaften, Berlin, 1965, 53. Hereafter referred to as *Macek I*.

[5] *Ibid.*, 69.

[6] *Ibid.*, 25, 28.

[7] *Ibid.*, 69-70.

[8] *Ibid.*, 62.

tensive copper and silver mines second in importance only to agri-culture.[9] Even though in 1525 these had been almost totally mort-gaged to the great banking houses, they still represented an economic advantage which other Europeans did not enjoy, and somewhat eased the burden of the subjects.

In Tyrol, as elsewhere therefore, the relatively higher level of prosperity seems to have been part of the cause of the revolt. The concern not to lose the advantages gained certainly heightened the level of dissatisfaction with the tendency of the government and the nobility to restrict the freedoms and the greater material well-being of the peasants.

Still, while there were wealthy and well-to-do farmers in Tyrol, the majority of the population consisted of poorer farmers, renters with not enough land to feed their families, and the chronically poor farm help. In the towns the wage earners, members of the small guilds, mercenary footsoldiers, and journeymen made up the mass of the poor. All these together constituted what was referred to in contemporary documents as the *Pofl*.[10] In the towns the poor frequent-ly represented a considerable percentage of the population. They were therefore a factor seriously to be reckoned with in times of social upheaval.

The thesis that the major cause of the revolt in Tyrol was the in-tolerable weight of oppression on the peasants is unassailable. For the people on the land were more and more oppressed by a nobility that found itself increasingly in economic trouble. The indiscriminate crea-tion of knights and the growing devotion to luxurious living pro-portionately reduced the wealth available to each.[11] The almost com-pleted obsolescence of armoured cavalry and its replacement by the *Landsknecht* infantry made up of farmers and townspeople added to the insecurity of the nobility, for it called in question their privileged position.[12] Their economic and social insecurity was reflected in ever increasing pressure on their subjects.

The number and level of ordinary and extraordinary rents, taxes, and levies laid on the tenant farmers was staggering. The two basic assessments were the rent in kind or in money to the landlord and

---

[9] *Ibid.*, 44-45.

[10] Pofl: Pöbel: rabble. *Macek I*, 55.

[11] Paul von Hoffman, "Geschichte Tirols von 1523-1526: Der Tiroler Bauern-aufstand," Innsbruck, typewritten diss. 1948, Universität Innsbruck, 1-2.

[12] H. Wopfner, *Die Lage Tirols zu Ausgang des Mittelalters und die Ursachen des Bauernkrieges*, Berlin-Leipzig, 1908, 81.

the great tithe to the church. To this was added the small tithe which was levied on animals, gardens, flocks of poultry, or other small sources of production needed for the family's food supply.[13] There were special levies for the dogs, kitchen, and castle watch of the landlord.[14] Work levies for the upkeep of castles and roads at the convenience of the lord were common.[15] Other extraordinary levies were the Leap Year rent which was an extra annual rent every fourth year,[16] a special interest on long-standing debts,[17] a tax on taking over or terminating a lease which could be as much as ten percent of the value of the property leased,[18] and the heriot (a steer if the tenant died; a cow for the tenant's wife).[19] The practice of annual lease (*Freistift*), widespread in the south, was especially onerous since the rent could be fixed arbitrarily by the landlord every year. Often the rent ran to over fifty percent.[20] Indirectly the farmers were affected by the gradual usurpation of the common rights of pasture, wood-cutting, hunting, and fishing by the feudal lords.[21] Payment of tithes was frequently required even if there was no produce due to drought, storm, or flood.[22] On top of all that were the recurring heavy levies on part of the sovereign for the conduct of the endless wars against France, Venice, and the Turks. While the nobles and the clergy were subject to this tax as well, they had ways of passing the weight of it on to their subjects.[23] Economic oppression was thus also a cause of the revolt.

Another important cause was Ferdinand's determination to intro-

[13] G. Franz, *Quellen zur Geschichte des Bauernkrieges*, Darmstadt: Wissenschaftliche Buchgesellschaft, 1963, 282, 271; Tiroler Geschichtsquellen III, Innsbruck: Tiroler Landesarchiv, 1976, 8.

[14] *Ibid.*, 279.

[15] H. Wopfner, *Quellen zur Geschichte des Bauernkrieges in Deutschtirol 1525. I. Teil: Quellen zur Vorgeschichte des Bauernkrieges: Beschwerdeartikel aus den Jahren 1519-1525*, Innsbruck, 1908, 145-147; Franz, *Quellen*, 279; *TGQ*, 20, 47, 61, 73, 77.

[16] Franz, *Quellen*, 279.

[17] *Ibid.*, 281.

[18] *Ibid.*, 280; *TGQ*, 3, 6, 15, 32, 40.

[19] Wopfner, *Die Lage Tirols*, 37-47; J. Macek, "Zu den Anfängen des Tiroler Bauernkrieges. Der Landtag der Bauern in Meran und die Meraner Artikel," *Historica I*, 1960, 172-3. Hereafter referred to as *Macek II*; *TGQ*, 2-3, 5-6, 28, 36, 69, 75.

[20] Wopfner, *Die Lage Tirols*, 45; *Macek I*, 61.

[21] *Macek I*, 62-4; Franz, *Quellen*, 277, 283; *TGQ*, 3, 4, 5, 8, 9-10, 13, 14-15, 20, 25-26, 29, 51.

[22] *TGQ*, 17, 19, 22, 23, 27, 33-34, 39-40, 41, 44, 48, 57, 74.

[23] *Macek I*, 65. Even this enumeration is not complete. See the cited works, especially *Macek I*, for other exactions.

duce Roman law, a policy which was designed to centralize his power and the administration of his domains.[24] The peasant submissions of grievance beginning in 1519 repeatedly complain about the violations of ancient rights. Especially irksome was the appointment of judicial officials without consultation,[25] and the attempted centralization of the judiciary, which created uncertainty about the procurement of justice not to speak of the inconvenience of greater travelling distance.[26] A further complaint was that the judiciary introduced various novelties in judicial procedure which represented a burden to the people.[27]

This attempted replacement of common law by Roman law left the peasant very uncertain as to the continuance of his traditional rights and led to his appeal to the old law (*das alte Recht*). Faced with lawyers trained in Roman law who came to have more and more influence in Innsbruck and the smaller administrative centres, the peasant could no longer defend himself against the claims of his lord and grew more and more resentful of the legal process.[28] Moreover the new legal procedures with their mystification of legal jargon and method were a ready source of funds for the authorities, since they charged high fees for any legal transactions.[29] This only served to heighten the anger and frustration of the peasant.

A common grievance related to the stranglehold which the great commercial companies had upon the economy of the country. Typical is a poem which appeared in April, 1525, in which the Fuggers are identified as one of the five villains that will have to be gotten rid of before things get better in Tyrol.[30] The Fuggers held leases on a number of silver and copper mines in return for large loans to Maximilian I and Ferdinand I.[31] The Fuggers were also among the companies that speculated in wares, buying up quantities of goods and then selling at high prices when scarcity set in. This practice was

---

[24] Wopfner, *Die Lage Tirols*, 188; *Macek I*, 65. See also G. Franz, *Der Deutsche Bauernkrieg*, 1-2.

[25] Wopfner, *Quellen*, 8-9, 121, 147, 191; *TGQ*, 17, 45-46.

[26] *Ibid.*, 14, 23-24.

[27] *Ibid.*, 160; *TGQ*, 22, 24, 28, 31-32, 38, 67-68, 71.

[28] Theodor von Kern, "Zur Geschichte der Volksbewegung in Tirol 1525," *AGAT I*, 1865, 92-95. Cf. Cf. Abraham Friesen, *The Marxist Interpretation of the Reformation*, University Microfilms, 1967, p. 365 and Günther Franz, *op. cit.*, 2.

[29] *Macek I*, 64-65.

[30] Kern, *op. cit.*, 94.

[31] See *Macek I*, 45-49.

particularly onerous and contributed to special hardship when staple foods were involved.[32]

Yet another major cause of the peasant revolt in Tyrol was the deplorable state of the church, especially as represented by the clergy. Josef Egger, a 19th century Tyrolian historian, claimed that the aim of the peasants around Brixen was to get rid of the old faith.[33] It is quite likely that Wopfner's judgement that the majority of the people felt basically satisfied in the old church is the more accurate.[34] Removal of the worst abuses would have assured their religious loyalty. As with the general social and economic conditions, so conditions in the church had reached a critical point in 1525. On the basis of its visible manifestation little that is positive can be reported.[35]

Most of the Tyrol fell to the sees of Brixen and Trent with some smaller areas going to the archbishopric of Salzburg and to the diocese of Chur. As elsewhere, the church had vast real estate holdings in Tyrol, which came to not less than thirty-three percent of the total arable land.[36] Most of this was rented on an hereditary (*Erblehen*) or tempo-rary (*Freistift*) basis.[37] Generally the tenants on church lands were less independent than elsewhere and were economically worse off.[38] The limited cases of serfdom were in the jurisdiction of the bishop of Chur.

The two prince-bishops, Sebastian Sprentz of Brixen and Bernhard von Cles of Trent were both more prince and less bishop.[39] Both

---

[32] H. Wopfner, "Bozen im Bauernkriege von 1525," *Der Schlern V*, 1924, 147; *Die Lage Tirols*, 33; *TGQ*, 6, 2, 40, 50.

[33] J. Egger, *Geschichte Tirols von den ältesten Zeiten bis in die Neuzeit*. II. Bd. Innsbruck, 1876, 94.

[34] Wopfner, *Die Lage Tirols*, 94. Cf. Bernd Moeller, "Piety in Germany Around 1500," *The Reformation in Medieval Perspective*, ed. Steven E. Ozment, Chicago: Quadrangle Books, 1971.

[35] Although see Martin Kiem, "Zeitgemässe Besprechungen geschichtlicher Ereignisse. Die Glaubensspaltung im 16. Jhd. in Tirol," *Tirolensien III. Separat-abdrücke aus Artikeln des Tiroler Volksblatt* Jg. 90/91, 1892. For a general discussion of the state of church and clergy see J. Lortz, *Die Reformation in Deutschland*, Vol. X, Herder, 1962, pp. 73-96. Although that deals more specifically with Germany its basic assertions may be taken to apply to Tyrol as well. Cf. *Luther, Erasmus and the Reformation*, ed. J. C. Olin *et al*. New York, 1969, p. 80.

[36] Wopfner, *Die Lage Tirols*, 3.

[37] Wopfner, "Bozen im Bauernkriege von 1525," 146.

[38] Wopfner, *Die Lage Tirols*, 90.

[39] Jörg Kirchmair, "Denkwürdigkeiten," *Fontes rerum austriacarum*, 1855, 461.

"Der bischof von Triennt wie vnverporgen ist, hett seinem stift nit vast wol gehaust. Dan er ye ain fursten Diener lieber dan ain bischof sein wolt; damit er vil verthat, hoffte doch teglich der furst solt Ime des widerumb ergetzen. Und nachdem der sprenntz Bischof zu prichsen nicht befreunttet oder von adl was, vermaint er Im ainen Ruggn pey dem furstn zemachen. Vnd pey disem gunst suechen vergassen sy des gemainen Nutz gemainer Lantschaft vast gar."

were fabulously wealthy [40] and trusted counsellors of Ferdinand I.
Consequently they spent much of their time in Innsbruck,[41] giving
relatively little attention to the growing volume of complaints about
church abuses and even less to doing anything about them.[42] Both
men were among the five mentioned in the anonymous poem of 1525
that were to be removed for the good of the land.[43]

The chronicler Kirchmair, himself a devoted churchman, complained that Sprentz had enough to do at home without always run-
ning off to Innsbruck.[44] A survey of general conditions proves him
right. There was a critical shortage of parish clergy.[45] All too often
the incumbent of a parish did not reside there [46] and simply appointed
a vicar to perform his duties who was paid a very low stipend.[47] This
led to a constant turnover of priests going from one place to another
to improve their living.[48] Many of them came from abroad, had no
knowledge of language and local conditions, and thus only worsened
an already grave situation. And as if that were not enough, many of
these priests had proved unfit for their office elsewhere and now
functioned in Tyrol, often unknown to the bishops.[49] Many of them
were completely ignorant.[50] Because of the frequently insufficient

---

[40] *Macek I*, 24.

[41] Wopfner, *Die Lage Tirols*, 91.

[42] F. A. Sinnacher, *Beyträge zur Geschichte der bischoflichen Kirchen Säben und
Brixen in Tirol*, Vol. VII, 1830, 178-180, 191-192, 197, 199-200. J. Bücking claims
that the bishops in Tyrol actually had only very limited room for action in church
reform because the sovereign had gathered the power of initiative and approval
extensively into his own hands. ("Reformation und Katholische Reform in Tirol,"
Der Schlern, 45, 1971, 130-132).

[43] Kern, *op. cit.*

[44] Kirchmair, *op. cit.*, 465.

[45] Egger, *op. cit.* II, 77; G. Mecenseffy, *Geschichte des Protestantismus in Österreich*,
Graz-Köln, 1956, 6. Actually there was an oversupply of priests making up as
much as one-third of the population in some places. Most of these priests did
nothing but read the masses for the dead and thus constituted an additional
economic burden. (Bücking, *op. cit.*, 128).

[46] This was the case with the parish of Hall of which Dr. Ambros Iphover was
the pastor. He resided at Brixen where he was one of the canons of the Cathedral.
Gustav Bosserts, "Beiträge zur Geschichte Tirols in der Reformationszeit,"
Jahrbuch der Gesellschaft für die Geschichte des Protestantismus in Österreich 6, 1844, 156.
Hereafter referred to as *JGGPÖ*.

[47] Egger, *op. cit.* II, 78.

[48] Anselm Sparber, *Kirchengeschichte Tirols*, Innsbruck, 1957, 47.

[49] Egger, *op. cit.* II, 77.

[50] A poem concerning the clergy that was current in Tyrol in 1525 went as
follows:

> Man schätzt die Priesterschaft gering,
> als ob sie wär ein leichtes Ding.

stipend priests were driven to seek other sources of income. Thus they came to charge fees for dispensing communion, for burial, for giving absolution.[51] Some ran stands for the sale of brandy adjacent to the church to add to their income.[52]

But even these conditions might not have caused the general and deep-seated anticlericalism of the time had it not been for the morally objectionable behaviour of many of the clergy from the highest prelate to the lowliest vicar. Ecclesiastical benefice was widely viewed as a means of financial enrichment. A question commonly asked about a vacant benefice was "What does it pay in absentia?" Complaints about lazy, drinking, gaming priests were common, as also about the keeping of concubines.[53] Although the bishops of Brixen attempted to initiate some reforms they achieved little.[54] Generally even the will for reform was lacking. The actual attitude of the higher clergy was revealed in their reply to grievances against them sumbitted to the Diet of 1525. They rejected the complaints which were based on common knowledge and experience as totally unproven and therefore unjustified.[55] All they seemed capable of doing by way of response to the disaffection of the people was to insist on the obligation of faithfully observing even the smallest cultic provision as necessary for eternal salvation.[56]

The fact that the clergy were not subject to civil law like everyone else and thus enjoyed distinct advantages added to anticlerical sentiment. Moreover the clergy were exempt from a number of tolls and levies along with the nobility. This gave them a commercial advantage

---

Drum findet man jetzt junge Pfaffen,
die nicht mehr können als die Affen,
und Seelsorg nehmen Leut auf sich,
denen man kaum vertraut ein Viech . . .

Hans Benedikter, *Rebell im Land Tirol: Michael Gaismair*, Wien, 1970, 40.

[51] Egger, *op. cit.*, 78.

[52] Mecenseffy, *op. cit.*, 6.

[53] Wopfner, *Die Lage Tirols*, 87. Although Kiem, *op. cit.*, attacks Egger's description of the state of the church, his own evaluation in fact supports Egger's basic contentions. See also *Macek I*, 29 and G. Loesche, "Archivalische Beiträge zur Geschichte des Täufertums und des Protestantismus in Tirol und Vorarlberg," *JGGPÖ*, 47, 1926, X.

[54] Kiem, *op. cit.*, 179-181.

[55] L'archivio di Stato Bolzano (ASB), *Cassa 38*, no. 10.

"Vom ersten in dem eingang zeigen si an, wie in beden, geistlichen vnd weltlichn stand sich vil missbrauch erhebt, des ain erwurdig briesterschaft nit gesteet, ist das auf diese stund nit bewisen."

[56] Bossert, *op. cit.*, 156.

for example in the production and sale of wine.[57] The universal demand of the peasants to choose their own pastors must be seen as one means of controlling clerical privilege.[58]

"A similar sad wasteland was observable in the area of charity," writes Joseph Hirn, late 19th century Tyrolian historian. In the fifteenth century much had been done for suffering humanity by way of pious foundations for aid to the poor. But the sixteenth century "almost completely lacks this most attractive practical fruit of true christianity." In fact much that had been established in the fifteenth century died of neglect or of even worse illness in the sixteenth.[59] The monasteries, which had performed much of this function were in as deplorable a state as the rest of the church. The chronicler Kirchmair writes about the luxurious living in the ancient New Abbey,[60] and in a letter to bishop Sprentz he requests the absent bishop to admonish the monks to attend to divine worship, to curb their sexual appetites, and to conduct themselves uprightly. If there is no improvement, he continues, they will get a manager who will not send them *to* church but will kick them *out* of it.[61] The basic complaint again and again is that the clergy from the pope down run after wealth and care nothing for the flock entrusted to them.[62] The common people, preserving an innate sense of the propriety of things, therefore accepted whatever weapons were offered them to resist the oppression of the church.

Such a weapon was the new evangelical preaching which emanated from Wittenberg and Zürich. Jakob Strauss was the first Lutheran preacher to settle in Tyrol. He also preached in Hall where he was succeeded after one year by Urban Rhegius who, like Strauss, was expelled by the authorities.[63] Their teaching was very critical of the clergy and the authoritarian claims of church and state. Thousands accepted their teaching. In 1523 a tailor's apprentice from the Puster valley began to preach around Brixen claiming that the people have

---

[57] *Macek I*, 30.

[58] "Beschwerden der Bauernschaft an der Etsch," *Tiroler Landesregierungs Archiv (TLRA), Tirolische Empörung (TE)*, 58.

[59] Hirn, *Erzherzog Ferdinand II von Tirol. Geschichte Seiner Regierung und Seiner Länder*. I. Bd., Innsbruck, 1885, 75.

[60] Kirchmair in a letter to bishop Sprentz printed in the introduction to *Denkwürdigkeiten*, XX; also 476.

[61] *Ibid.*

[62] *Macek I*, 29.

[63] *Ibid.*, 78-80.

all been deceived by the pope, monks, and priests.[64] The following year a priest from the Ziller valley was preaching sermons from the pulpit and in the taverns that were critical of the church and hierarchy.[55] When he was imprisoned in Kropfsberg Castle a mob of local residents gathered at the castle to liberate him by force.[66] In 1525 there is report of a monk who laid aside his habit and was working as a miner at Schwaz and at the same time spreading Lutheran teaching.[67] Lutheran views were defended by monks in the large and influential monastery at Stams, and when the authorities from Innsbruck went to investigate, they found themselves facing a large crowd of angry farmers and townspeople who came to defend the offenders.[68] Lutheran books were openly sold on the market in Hall contrary to decrees issued against such practice.[69] The first decree, issued on November 6, 1523, had already to be repeated on April 22, 1525.[70] Another decree directed against the dissemination of Lutheran teaching [71] and issued following the Diet of Regensburg clearly reveals Ferdinand's determination to carry out the Edict of Worms.[72] Nonconformists were vigorously proceeded against, and the severity of the penalties was likely one of the causes contributing to the outbreak of the revolt.[73] The episcopal zeal for the purity of the church expressed in the persecution was hard to reconcile with their general worldly conduct and the people refused to accept the glaring contradiction.[74]

The revolt in Tyrol was therefore brought on by at least four causes. The main one was the economic oppression of the peasant. The peasant grievance submissions between 1519 and 1525 clearly demonstrate this even though the lot of the Tyrolian peasant was generally better than elsewhere. A second cause was the fear of the centralization of power by means of Roman law which would annul ancient

---

[64] K. Sinzinger, *Das Täufertum im Pustertal*, Diss. Univ. of Innsbruck, 1950, 76.
[65] *TLRA, Causa Domini* I (*CD*), 113f.
[66] *Ibid.*, 116f.
[67] *Ibid.*, 127f. See also 111v.
[68] *TLRA An die Fürstliche Durchlaucht* I (*AFD*), 219.
[69] *TLRA CD I*, 30v.
[70] *Ibid.*, 93.
[71] "Lutheran" is the term used at this time for any teaching critical of the Catholic Church. It could also mean Zwinglian. Later records even refer to Lutheran Anabaptists, which is a complete contradiction.
[72] *Ibid.*, 134 plus 9 unnumbered pages.
[73] Egger, *op. cit.* II, 91; Franz, *Der Deutsche Bauernkrieg*, 1933, 257.
[74] *Ibid.*, 88.

rights and privileges. Thirdly there was the resentment at control of the economy by foreign commercial and banking interests. Finally, a fourth major cause was the deepseated dissatisfaction and frustration with the abuses that afflicted the church. Had serious alleviation of these in whole or in part been carried out the revolt could have been avoided. But the people who were expected to make the necessary changes were the ones who benefitted from the abuses. A revolt was therefore inevitable.

2. GAISMAIR'S DEVELOPMENT INTO A REVOLUTIONARY

Michael Gaismair was born between 1485 and 1490 in the village of Tschöfs above Sterzing along the road to the Brenner.[75] His grandfather had been a farmer. His father, Jacob Gaismair, had worked his way up to relative prosperity in a mining enterprise, and had even purchased a farm in the Pflersch Valley near Tschöfs.[76] Michael Gaismair was thus born into a well-to-do home and would hardly have known poverty at first hand. The subsequent official positions which Gaismair held likely indicate that this father had planned such a career for his son. Where he got the education for his career is not certain. He may have attended the Cathedral school in Brixen as Macek strongly suggests,[77] or perhaps more likely, the Latin school in Sterzing as Sparber supposes.[78] Sparber is probably right since, as he suggests, the youth would most likely have attended the school nearest the family home.

Which were the influences that made a religious and social nonconformist out of Gaismair? Macek suggests that he may have come under the influence of the still lingering humanism and reformism of Nicholas of Cusa, and that this helped to develop critical thinking and shape his views about the necessity of church reform.[79] This may be correct, but the case would depend on the proof that Cusa's influence was still noticeably in evidence. Macek does not offer such proof. Anselm Sparber, by contrast, says that Nicholas of Cusa left no good memories in Brixen. The people sided with Sigmund in the feud between the two, and the cardinal's death was regarded as a deliverance

---

[75] E. Auckenthaler, "Michael Gaismair's Heimat und Sippe," *Der Schlern* 21, 1947, 18.
[76] *Macek I*, 144-145.
[77] *Ibid.*, 146.
[78] "Geschichte des Bauernaufstandes in Tirol von 1525", *Dolomiten* Dec. 4, 1968, 10.
[79] *Macek I*, 146.

for Brixen and Tyrol.[80] The claim that a positive influence lingered can therefore well be questioned.

Not enough information about the early life of Michael Gaismair is available to say anything about the roots of his evolution into a revolutionary. We must look for clues to this process during the period of his employment as secretary of Leonhard von Völs, the vice-regent of Tyrol, and of Sebastian Sprentz, bishop of Brixen. In the employ of these two men he developed his passion for social justice and his rejection of the church as a corrupt institution. We know enough about Gaismair's two employers to be able to draw some conclusions from their activity for his development into a revolutionary.

Gaismair may, as Macek suggests, have come into the employ of Leonhard von Völs through the efforts of his father who had contacts with the royal administration in Innsbruck.[81] Until now the only contemporary reference to Gaismair's services to the vice-regent came from *Franz Schweyger's Chronik der Stadt Hall*,[82] which merely mentions the fact but gives no other information. To this can now be added a short note from the financial records of the government at Innsbruck which reveals that an amount of money was paid to Michael Gaismair for secretarial services at the Diet of 1523.[83] Gaismair must have married about the year 1507 [84] and likely entered upon his career about the same time.

Leonhard von Völs became vice-regent in the year 1499. The position was a royal appointment with a salary paid by the sovereign. But while the vice-regent was appointed to look after the interests of the sovereign, he was also given to the people of Tyrol as a kind of

---

[80] "Vom Wirken des Kardinals Nikolaus von Cues als Fürstbischof von Brixen (1450-1464)", *Veröffentlichungen des Museum Ferdinandeum*, 26/29, 1946-1949, 378.
[81] *Macek I*, 145, 147.
[82] *Franz Schweger's Chronik der Stadt Hall 1303-1572* ed. D. Schönherr, 1867, 88.
[83] TLRA *Raitbuch 1523*, 144. In spite of an exhaustive search of all the official records in the TLRA and the Ferdinandeum in Innsbruck from 1510-1523, as well as of the Episcopal archives (L'archivio vescovile) in Brixen, not a single further reference to Gaismair's life prior to May 1525 could be found. An attempt at determining the dates of Gaismair's employment with Bishop Sprentz by comparison of handwriting proved inconclusive because of the similarity of secretarial handwritings. It may be that when the new South Tyrol archives are set up in Bolzano more information will be available.
[84] This inference follows from the assumptions regarding Gaismair's age discussed in note 148 below. Beda Weber writes that he was married early to a strong, vain woman, without however giving any documentation for it (*Die Stadt Bozen*, 1849, 78).

ombudsman, a protector of their liberties over against the sovereign.[85] The information we have about the highranking noble and royal official Leonhard von Völs, however, suggests almost unanimously that he did not fit that definition of the office. In fact, one of the Meran Articles of 1525 calls for the abolition of the office altogether since "Lienhart von Vels' attitude toward the people has been such ... that we do not want him nor anyone else as vice-regent henceforth." [86] Already in 1520 in the wake of Maximilian's death his own subjects had told him that they would not obey him, for they were waiting for the Emperor,[87] indicating that they had more confidence in the distant emperor as champion of their rights than in the present imperial "ombudsman."

The complaints of his subjects in Meran, Völs, Kastelruth, Tiers, and Salurn submitted against him to the Diet of Innsbruck in 1525 include almost every complaint voiced by peasants against their feudal lords in Tyrol in that year. According to these he made it very difficult for his subjects to achieve justice in legal cases, so much so that some claimed to be better off simply to suffer loss. The subjects of Meran complain that he always is at his castle of Prösels beyond Bozen, but even the poor man has to go there to get a hearing at greater expenses than he can afford.[88]

Thus the subjects of Salurn request the right to stay in lodgings of their own choice when they come to attend a hearing and not to have to pay the higher rates charged by Leonhard von Völs.[89] There are complaints about raising rents against ancient usage,[90] and especially frequent are the charges that he has against all justice taken for his own use common pasture land either by fencing it in, or turning it into ponds for raising fish.[91] So many levies of labour were laid on the subjects of Salurn that they had difficulty looking after their own

[85] J. Ladurner, "Die Landeshauptleute von Tirol," *AGAT* II, 1865, 3, 9. See also J. Hirn, *Die Entwickelung der Landeshauptmannswürde in Tirol und die Familie Brandis*, Innsbruck, 1892, 1-3.

[86] Franz, *Quellen*, 276 (art. 14) "Dann sich Herr Lienhart von Vels dermassen gegen ainer Landschaft gehalten, ... das man weder ihn noch ander furon kain Landhauptman mer haben will. ..."

[87] F. Hirn, *Geschichte der Tiroler Landtage 1518 bis 1521*, Freiburg i. B. 1905, 33.

[88] Wopfner, *Quellen*, 153, 139, 145, 90. The traditional seat of the vice-regent was castle Tyrol near Meran.

[89] *Ibid.*, 147.

[90] *Ibid.*, 153, 154, 148.

[91] *Ibid.*, 153, 147.

harvests.[92] Unfair measuring practices, special taxes on labourers, interference with commercial practices to his own benefit, and still other complaints complete the list.[93] Several letters to Leonhard von Völs by Bishop Sebastian Sprentz support the charges of arbitrary interference in the rights of the people. In one letter the bishop specifically says that the action in question prejudiced the honour of the office of vice-regent.[94]

Gaismair was *Landschreiber an der Etsch*, that is, he discharged the secretarial services dealing specifically with the office of the vice-regent. That means he worked at Prösels Castle and regularly accompanied the vice-regent to the annual Diet.[95] In this role he had ample opportunity to get well acquainted with conditions in the land as well as with many people. But he also saw the constant perversion of justice, the continual oppression of the poor, the arbitrary actions in pursuit of advantage by his employer. For example, in one case, when a farmer would not be silenced in his objection to the lord's high-handed building of a watercourse across his land, von Völs summarily imposed a high fine and prison sentence on the man.[96] Gaismair saw the poor people being molested by the castle personnel,[97] saw a tenant bringing a levy of chickens and being told that they were not fat enough, and year after year observed the peasants at work at the castle cleaning, weeding, removing snow from the roofs, and bringing up large quantities of wood and wine.[98]

Beda Weber reports that on the margin of the official minutes of a legal case in the Bolzano archives, he discovered the following notations in Gaismair's own hand:

> "I suffer in silence and wait,
> As I remember their innocence,"
> "No good remains unrewarded;

---

[92] *Ibid.*, 145, 146, 147.

[93] *Ibid.*, 145, 153, 90.

[94] AVB *RN*, letters dated Apr. 12, Apr/May, 1522 and Aug. 12, 1523, fol. 285-287, 321-323, 610-611. Further evidence that von Völs interfered with the regular course of justice comes from letters of Charles V and Ferdinand I to him in which he is sternly charged to observe the laws (BFTD *Codex 1182*; letters dated Jan. 2, 1521 and Sept. 10, 1523).

[95] TLRA *Raitbuch 1523*, 144. "Micheln Gayssmair lanndschreiber an der etsch auss g[egebe]n für sein schreiben und mue so er in jungstgehalten lantag hie gethan. . . ."

[96] Wopfner, *Quellen*, 153.

[97] *Ibid.*

[98] *Ibid.*, 145-146.

No evil unavenged."
"One can get far by going slow." [99]

Since the records Weber mentions were in Bolzano it may be safe
to assume that they came from nearby Prösels where Leonhard von
Völs spent most of his time, and where therefore Gaismair himself
worked. If these comments are from Gaismair's hand—and there is
no good reason to suppose they are not—they say a great deal about
him. They reveal that even before he moved to Brixen he had resolved
to do something about the injustice he observed every day. Günther
Franz comments on those jottings as follows: "These notations
characterize his attitude: a sense of justice like that of the Old Testament, tough, goal-directed determination and sympathy with the oppressed people which was the innocence he wanted to rescue." [100]
Here at the seat of injustice, he acquired his remarkable knowledge of
the law of Tyrol, for it was at Prösels that the Tyrolian "Bill of
Rights", the document that detailed the privileges of the Tyrolian
estates, was kept.[101] It can be assumed that, since Gaismair also kept
minutes of legal cases, he had thoroughly familiarized himself with
the contents of these ancient documents. It was here that his determination to see those principles of justice prevail ripened in him. It
may well be that even in those days—six, seven, ten years before 1525?
—he was talking to people and becoming known as one who was concerned about the plight of the oppressed. And what more convenient
way to contact people from all over Tyrol and beyond than at the
four annual fairs in Bozen nearby, which, according to a Trentine
document of 1486 was the "Emporium of the German and Italian
nations"?[102] Here he could have talked to the servants in the retinues
of the merchants from Italy, Germany, Switzerland, and the rest of
Austria. This may also have been the route by which he first became
acquainted with the new religious ideas emanating from Wittenberg
and Zürich since 1520. Another piece of evidence that Gaismair was

[99] B. Weber, *Die Stadt Bozen*, 1849, 78. Unfortunately Weber does not document
his claim. See *Macek I*, 147, note 98.
   "Ich leid' und schweig' und trag Geduld mit aller Unschuld."
   "Es bleibt kein Gutes unbelohnt, kein Übles ungerochen."
   "Langsam geht man auch weit."
[100] Franz, *Der Deutsche Bauernkrieg*, 157. Writer's translation. "Diese Sprüche
kennzeichnen sein Wesen: ein fast alttestamentliches Rechtsbewusstsein, zähe,
zielbewusste Entschlossenheit und Mitleid mit dem unterdrückten Volk, dass für
ihn die Unschuld war, die er retten wollte."
[101] See note 169 below.
[102] Otto Stolz, "Die Bozner Messe," *Südtirol* (Oct. 1948, 1), 22.

even then talking to people about social justice may be the fact that another secretary of Leonhard von Völs was reported as a Gaismair follower in 1527, and yet a third, Michael Kürschner, later became a prominent Tyrolian Anabaptist leader.[103] Perhaps Gaismair and others in the secretarial office at Prösels had reached a mutual understanding to act together against injustice.

It may be assumed that Gaismair was at this time an unquestioning adherent of the old Church for there is no evidence of the new Reformation teaching coming into Tyrol before 1520. Other interpreters have assumed too readily that Gaismair's views about the equal rights of all men to justice were based on Reformation teaching. This need not have been so since it was entirely possible for the Catholic tradition to ignite and nourish the demand for social justice based on the equality of all men. One has only to point to the earlier peasant uprisings in Europe which were always demands for justice, especially after 1512 when the call for "divine justice" (*göttliche Gerechtigkeit*) became a major component of peasant programs. Günther Franz cites the specific case of a monk in Graz in 1478 who publicly posted an appeal to the Emperor to give justice to the poor who are the bloody victims of the rich and powerful. The poor have no rights, and therefore, without delay, the Emperor must be reconciled to them. For without their love his wickedness will plunge him into the abyss of hell.[104] There was also the so-called "*oberrheinische Revolutionär,*" a radical reform tract from between 1502 and 1513 which insists that the farmer has the same blood as the nobleman, and that by natural and divine right he ought not any longer to be oppressed. The mighty have forfeited their right to rule. Thus a new ruler will be elected by the people who will "put away the flail and the hoe and take up the iron [weapon] to resist presumption, promote the common good, and give a hand to the Word of God." [105]

In 1439 the so-called *Reformatio Sigismundi* appeared, a writing suffused with the notion of the divine law. The author despairs of the

---

[103] Confession of Michael Gall, Sept. 1527, TLRA *HR 106*, 190-191.

[104] Franz, *Der Deutsche Bauernkrieg*, 58-59.

[105] *Ibid.*, 114-115. For an English translation of excerpts see G. Strauss, *Manifestations of Discontent*, Bloomington, Ind.: University of Indiana Press, 1971, pp. 233-247. Translation based on *Das Buch der Hundert Kapitel und der Vierzig Statuten des sogenannten Oberrheinischen Revolutionärs*, ed. Gerhard Zschäbitz and Annelore Franke, Berlin, 1967. For the influence of this work and the Reformatio Sigismundi on the peasant movement see Hartmut Boockman, "Zu den geistigen und religiösen Voraussetzungen des Bauernkrieges", *Bauernkriegsstudien*, hrg. B. Moeller, Gütersloh: Gerd Mohn, 1975, 9-27.

possibility of justice being granted by those in power and warns that the poor will themselves see to the establishment of God's law. God has delivered man from all bondage and no one may now enslave another man. Anyone who does so should be forcibly got rid of.[106] Most of the printings of this work were done in Augsburg from where they could come directly into Tyrol. It was reprinted several times during the years 1520-22.[107] Thus Gaismair could have had access to this work, especially since he lived within a few hours' ride of the famous Bozen fairs where the book would have been on sale.

All of this rested on a Catholic base and had fixed itself in receptive minds well before Luther's time. It is quite probable that Gaismair was one of these minds. This radical Catholic heritage would have been sufficient in and of itself to make a revolutionary of Michael Gaismair.

That late medieval heritage was now to be strenghtened by some of the ideas of the Protestant Reformation. Gaismair likely had his earliest personal contact with Reformation teaching while in the employ of Leonhard von Völs. Egger reports that the vice-regent was initially friendly to the new movement,[108] as were many of the higher nobility because of their hostility towards the church. Thus the perceptive secretary could easily have become exposed to the new ideas. But perhaps more important were the already mentioned annual fairs at Bozen. As soon as Reformation writings appeared they were sold in Bozen. The probing and inquisitive mind of Gaismair no doubt made the most of that opportunity. We hear of Lutheran books being sold at the fair in 1522,[109] which means that they had likely been in circulation even earlier. While the works of Luther that appeared in the years 1520-1524 were not intended to stimulate social revolution or to provide such a movement with an ideology, they did, to some extent, do just that. Luther's attack upon the Pope and the hierarchy put the ancient authorities in question and his writings about freedom of the Christian man were interpreted in social terms by the peasants. If one challenged the authority of Pope and prelate, the common people reasoned, why not of king and noble? And if every Christian was a priest, what further need was there for the clergy? Gaismair's own

---

[106] "Reformation Kaiser Sigmunds," ed. Heinrich Koller, *Monumenta Germaniae Historica* IV, Stuttgart, 1964, 84, 92, 168, 276-280, 57-58. For an English translation see Strauss, *op. cit.*, pp. 3-31.

[107] *Ibid.*, 26-27. *Macek II*, 191.

[108] Egger, *op. cit.*, II, 88.

[109] Weber, *op. cit.*, 75.

limited writing clearly shows that he did not separate the religious from the social as Luther did,[110] and there is no reason to suppose that he would have done it five years earlier. In any event, the so-called "Lutheran" preachers that worked in Brixen, Meran, and Bozen were much more socially radical than Luther himself. Thus, while Lutheran ideas doubtless influenced Gaismair, he can hardly have been a Lutheran in any recognizable form of that term. For him church reform and social reform went hand in hand and could in no wise be separated.

A source that could have formed this conviction in him during his time at Prösels was the Bible, especially the Old Testament. Beda Weber, early 19th century Tyrolian Benedictine scholar, states that German and Italian translations of the Bible were circulating among the people, and that by the time decrees against them were issued in 1523[111] they had long entered into the very heart of the nobility and the people.[112] Further it is wellknown that numerous German translations of the Bible or parts of it were available in print prior to Luther's translation. The Bozen fairs would have been the obvious source of such volumes. Perhaps Gaismair's conviction of the great importance of the Bible took root at this time. The Bible, and especially the Old Testament is the likeliest source for his towering sense of justice and of the pre-eminence of God's law over that of all human laws and institutions.

The continual observation of injustice on part of his employer and the influences of the radical Catholic social vision plus some Reformation teaching and preeminently the Bible combined to turn Gaismair into a prospective social revolutionary. His employment in the palace of prince-bishop Sebastian Sprentz would complete the process.

On April 9, 1521 Sebastian Sprentz was elected bishop of Brixen. Sprentz was a favourite of Cardinal Matthäus Lang of Salzburg,[113] who had evidently nominated his protege to the Emperor. Charles had ordered Leonhard von Völs and another Tyrolian noble to see to Sprentz's nomination in the Cathedral chapter. It is even possible that von Völs went to Brixen himself to see to the nomination.[114] Thus the Habsburgs had a firm supporter for their policies in the little prince-bishopric. Not everyone was pleased with this choice.

---

[110] See for example Luther's response to the Twelve Articles of the Peasants in *The Protestant Reformation* ed. Hans J. Hillerbrand, Harper & Row, 1968, 83-84.

[111] TLRA *CD* I, 48-49v.

[112] B. Weber, *Tirol und die Reformation*, Innsbruck, 1841, 49.

[113] Benedikter, *op. cit.*, 39.

[114] Sinnacher, *op. cit.*, VII, 181.

Especially indignant were a number among the nobility because an outsider had once again been appointed to a powerful position among them. There were, it was said, enough nobles and learned persons in the land that there was no need to resort to a stranger.[115] Sprentz himself wrote to Leonhard von Völs on June 27, 1521 to thank him for his influence in gaining the episcopate.[116] Although many nobles were opposed to Sprentz, von Völs seemed to have been on friendly terms with him to judge from the tone of their correspondence.[117]

It is therefore quite likely that Gaismair's move from the office of Leonhard von Völs to that of Bishop Sprentz of Brixen was arranged by these men.[118] Where in his previous employment Gaismair had seen the workings of a feudal estate with all of the oppression and perversion of justice so common throughout Europe in those days, he now saw not only a continuation of the same thing, since Sprentz was also a secular ruler and feudal lord, but also the inside story of the workings of a large diocese and its spiritual leader and shepherd. What he now observed can only have strengthened his determination to do something to set things right, and must have stiffened his opposition to the church and the clergy.

The overall impression one gets of Sebastian Sprentz from his personal correspondence is of a sincere man, determined to do what was right and lawful. The fact that he was a wealthy feudal lord should not a priori be used against him. His record as feudal lord is certainly much better than that of his friend Leonhard von Völs as well as of his fellow bishop Bernhard von Cles of Trent. As was to be expected of a man in his position, Sprentz looked after his own interests and safety first, and only secondarily after that of those committed to his care. When in January, 1522 upon his actual entry into Brixen he celebrated the pontifical high mass, only very few were allowed to attend since he was afraid of the plague which was raging in Brixen and the surrounding area just then.[119] This self-interest is also

---

[115] Egger, *op. cit.*, II, 84.

[116] Sinnacher, *op. cit.*, VII, 181. See AVB letter to Leonhard von Völs early Jan. 1522, *RN*, 155-156.

[117] See BTFD *Codex 1182*, letter of Sprentz to von Völs, July 23, 1521, and note 289 below.

[118] TLRA *Raitbuch 1523*, 144, indicates that on May 29, 1523 Gaismair was still in the employ of Leonhard von Völs.

[119] This is reported by Sinnacher *op. cit.*, VII, 127, based on *RN*, 155-156, although one ought to allow for the possibility that it was simply a measure to prevent further spreading of the plague. But when the peasant revolt broke out in Brixen, Sprentz, who was then in Innsbruck, fled in fear to a castle in Carniola.

supported by his record as feudal lord. His subjects appeared before him with petitions shortly after his arrival requesting alleviations of the heavy burden of levies and taxes. In his written response he promised to consider their complaints, but committed himself to no specification. He insisted in advance that he would not yield at points where his own income was concerned. He promised to charge his officials not to treat his subjects harshly.[120] In individual instances, therefore, he did demonstrate concern for his subjects, as when he ordered one of his supervisors to be lenient in demanding the rent because of a poor yield.[121] A number of instances demonstrate his concern for fair decision on part of his magistrates.[122]

On the other hand there is little doubt that he regarded his role as prince, royal counsellor, and feudal lord as more important than his function as bishop of a large diocese. A small indicator of this may be that of some twelve hundred pages of his extant episcopal administrative correspondence only seventeen pages are specifically referred to as dealing with spiritual matters. That he was absent when he was elected bishop was prophetic for the future.[123] Again and again he was unable to attend meetings called in the interests of church reform because his duties as secular lord were too pressing.[124] The chronicler Kirchmair gently censured his bishop by saying he would have had more than enough to do at home.[125] Certainly, considering the years of his episcopate in which Reformation teaching was further undermining the already shaky spiritual authority of the church, he was irresponsible and unresponsive to the crying demands for vigorous action to remove the abuses on which the new teaching fed. But in this Sprentz was no worse than most contemporary bishops.

If Gaismair knew the *Reformatio Sigismundi* he must now have un-

---

[120] *Ibid.*, 186-7. For specifics see AVB *RN*, 123-128, 129-131.

[121] AVB *RN*, 925.

[122] *Ibid.*, 118, 925, 77. The Text of the letter is as follows:

"Vnns gelangt sonst auch an Wie die leut vnd personen so vor dir als Richter schulden halben zuhandeln habn von dir gleich Recht vnd gericht nit bekomen mugen sondern dich darin verdachtlich haltest. Souerr dan dem also were so truegen wir nit vnbillich gross misfallen darob vnd wurden dardurch geursacht dermassen darein zusehen damit meniglich zu Recht vnd aller billikait komen mocht. Vnd Emphelhen dir demnach aber alen ernstlich das du dich in solhen vnd anderm val dermassen haltest als du dan von Ambtswegen deiner phlicht vnd ayd nach zutun schuldig bist."

[123] *Ibid.*, 179-180.

[124] *Ibid.*, 191-2, 193, 197, 199-200.

[125] Kirchmair, *op. cit.*, 465.

derstood why that author called for a complete abolition of the secular
power of the church,[126] for according to that writer the confusion of
the spiritual and secular authority was the cause for the deplorable
state of the church.[127] He must have seen how desperately the church
needed reform but looked in vain to its leaders to bring it about. He
must have seen clearly that his employer was so extensively concerned
with his secular role as prince and feudal lord that he really did not
have time to look after the spiritual welfare of his flock. Again Gaismair no doubt saw that there was an irreconcilable contradiction in
the assumption that a man could at the same time be both spiritual
father and feudal lord of the same people. Sprentz's credibility as a
spiritual guide acting in the name of Christ would necessarily be
undermined by his coercive practices as feudal lord. How could he
pronounce peace over his people and at the same time hold over them
the threat of retaliation by prison, torture, and death unless they
obeyed him? Evidently this was not felt to be a contradiction by the
bishops themselves or by most of the people of the sixteenth century.
But this fact cannot be marshalled to deny that people like Gaismair
did see the contradiction and that this conviction was important to
their proposals for a solution.[128]

All of these experiences and perceptions forced themselves upon
the discerning and sensitive secretary by the events in the bishop's
secular domain in early 1525. Ever since the beginning of peasant
unrest in Württemberg in late 1524 conditions were getting more and
more critical in Tyrol as well. Armed gatherings of farmers around
Brixen took place in 1524 and again in April, 1525. The bishop proceeded against the malcontents with the greatest severity. By his
vengeful action many of his flock were innocently tortured and in the
city of Brixen no fewer than forty-seven persons were executed within a period of three weeks.[129] Gaismair was probably present when the
two well-to-do farmers Balthasar Kefferer and Paul Pfefferer of New
Abbey were tried and condemned to a horrible, slow death on the
wheel.[130] Doubtless, since he worked in the *Hofburg* (bishop's castle)
he also had firsthand acquaintance with the case of Peter Pässler who,
because he had not been able to get what he considered justice ac-

---

[126] Koller, *op. cit.*, 230-232.
[127] *Ibid.*, 298.
[128] This can be plentifully documented from Anabaptist sources only a few
years later.
[129] Sinnacher, *op. cit.*, VII, 204.
[130] Kirchmair, *op. cit.*, 469.

cording to the ancient laws, had decided to get it by force, and had been arrested and imprisoned in the dungeon of that same fortress in Brixen in September, 1524. The trial dragged out through eight months at the end of which Pässler was condemned to death by fire. Gaismair knew that both the bishop and the court had refused pleas for mercy by Pässler's wife. Undoubtedly he knew of the popularity of Pässler among the population of the Puster and Eisack valleys.[131] Nor does it stretch credibility to suggest that Gaismair and Pässler were personal acquaintances although there is no evidence for it prior to May 13, 1525. If the assumption that Gaismair had for some years nurtured contacts with people in many parts of Tyrol is correct —and it is almost impossible to avoid such an assumption—it requires little imagination to understand what suffering he must have endured during those days in April, 1525. What self-control he must have exercised as secretary at the endless trials of people who were his friends! How the determination to avenge these wrongs must then have ripened awaiting only the convenient moment to act. As Hermann Holzmann writes: "One can understand Gaismair's chosen way only in view of much injustice and suffering [he saw], and as a consequence of terrible resentment." [132] The chosen way Holzmann refers to is of course Gaismair's fateful decision to follow the call of the Brixen rebels on May 13 to become their leader.

The review of the role of his employers in the development of his views and Gaismair's own notations on the margins of injustice [133] reveal a man who fervently believed in the inevitability of retribution for wrongs done and of reward for righteousness. Those are the ideas that come directly out of the biblical heritage in which it is especially emphasized that God, the final and just judge, is the champion of those who have been wronged. Because God holds in his own hands the reins of history the oppressed will be vindicated and the oppressors given their just penalty. When in the other notations he reflects the necessity for waiting he may be reflecting the biblical insistence that God waits to exercise his just vengeance until the cup of oppression and evil is full. Then the powerful who have wickedly a-bused their power will drink the cup of divine wrath. Finally his notations also imply a biblical sense of calling to be God's instrument of

[131] *Macek I*, 132-137.

[132] Hermann Holzmann, "Söhne der Heimat," *Schlern-Schriften* Bd. 232, 1965, 464.

[133] See page 16 above.

vengeance upon the wicked. He accepts his suffering and the necessity for quiet enduring patience until the time when God will bring
him out of seclusion and use him as the rod of retribution. It is not
by accident that Günther Franz refers to the Old Testament-like sense
of justice when commenting on Gaismair's notations.[134]

We may thus conclude that Gaismair had caught the biblical insistence that faithfulness to God consisted of exercising justice, loving
mercy, and walking humbly with God.[135] That in itself, as has happened so often in Christian history, would have made traditional
doctrinal and cultic orthodoxies appear in a new light. Their force and
authority would gradually have weakened in direct proportion to their
distance from the central concern for justice, mercy, and humility as
the principal demands of God. But this development does not imply
that Gaismair was now a Protestant of some persuasion, simply because these convictions were not characteristic of Protestantism at its
core any more than they were of Catholicism. Macek's statement
that Gaismair had grown up with the Reformation ideas of Luther
and Zwingli lacks all support.[136] That there were some Reformation
influences is granted but even for his later period he was evidently
selective. Luther as well as Zwingli would have rejected his Constitution as destructive. Gaismair must have continued to be at least
nominally Catholic, and perhaps at the same time advancing further
and further into a religious no-man's land which could not be clearly
identified by the traditional labels. It is possible that this venturing
away from the traditional religious moorings may have contributed
to the occasional uncertainty he felt about his role and his actions.

In summation therefore, while radical Catholic and Reformation
writings and ideas were available to all, they evidently lodged in the
receptive mind of Michael Gaismair and began working there. Why
they appealed to one person and not another, and why Gaismair's
mind was especially receptive toward them must remain hidden from
us.

3. The Tyrolian Revolt and Gaismair's Leadership

The revolt had almost broken out in 1520 in the wake of the death
of Maximilian I. The causes were those outlined above. There was a

---

[134] See note 100 above.
[135] Micah 6:8.
[136] "Das revolutionäre Programm des deutschen Bauernkriegs von 1526,"
Historica II, 1960, 113. Hereafter referred to as *Macek III*.

defiant mood abroad among the people and many resisted the oath of fealty.

The vice-regent was openly told by his tenants that they would not listen to him until the emperor appeared in Tyrol. At this time lack of common purpose among the people and a few token concessions to grievances united to prevent a full-scale uprising.[137] But the coals of discontent, anger, and insurrection continued to glow amid the combustible social conditions.[138] Early in 1525 Ferdinand managed to pacify the rebellious miners in North Tyrol conceding some of their demands.[139]

The unrest in the area of Brixen in the spring of 1525 met with the standard response of the tyrant. Within three weeks forty-seven persons were executed, among them the two wealthiest farmers of New Abbey. This cruelty on the part of the bishop filled the measure of resentment to overflowing.[140] That the authorities were fully occupied with the rising tide of anger and resentment may be indicated by the fact that the records of the daily transactions of the Brixen council minutes (*Rathsprotokoll*) end abruptly on May 6.[141] As is usually the case in such situations, one incident becomes the fuse which touched off the charge.

This incident was the rescue of Peter Pässler from execution. Pässler had turned Robin Hood when his father was deprived of his living by the bishop of Brixen. When all legal means failed to get him justice Peter took to the mountains, gathered a group of others in similar circumstances about him, and set about harassing the bishop and his officials, in order to get justice. He had many sympathizers in the Puster valley and elsewhere. The authorities made extensive efforts to apprehend him and in mid-summer 1524 they succeeded. Pässler was imprisoned in the bishop's fortress in Brixen until May 9, 1525, when the long, torturous process was over and he was to be executed. But when the bishop's soldiery led him the short distance from his prison to the block a consortium of angry and determined farmers rescued him and got him out of Brixen to safety.[142]

---

[137] *Macek I*, 114-117.

[138] Benedikter, *op. cit.*, 61-64.

[139] *Macek I*, 122, 126.

[14-] Benedikter, *op. cit.*, 64-65.

[141] Archivio vescovile Bressanone (AVB) *Rathsprotokoll de annis 1515-1527*, sections "Verhorpuech vnnd täglich beratschlagungen" and "Tagliche Handlungen vand Ratschleg auf Suplicacion de Anno 1525."

[142] AVB *Registrum notularum Sebastiani Sprenz Episcopi Brixinen De Annis 1521-1525* (RN), 943-948.

After that events moved quickly.[143] The citizens of Brixen made common cause with the peasants and on May 10 a force of armed men took over the city of Brixen, drove out the whole episcopal administrative apparatus, and plundered the houses of the cathedral canons. The bishop who was in Innsbruck at the time, fled to his castle Buchenstein near Cortina. On May 12 the insurgents plundered the wealthy New Abbey where that Georg Kirchmair, whose chronicle is a primary source for the events of those days, was magistrate and superintendent.[144] In a wild orgy of drunkenness and destruction the subjects of the Abbey wrought their vengeance on it for all the oppressions of the past. One of the leaders, Leonhard Püchler, stated that this was merely the beginning of what would happen. "To plunder the monasteries was a trivial matter. They would seize the castles and the watch towers in the land and turn a free country over to the sovereign. Nor did they intend any longer to pay taxes or levies. And if the sovereign did not agree to it he too would have to get out of the country." [145]

The next day, May 13, the sober realities of the situation led the rebels to elect a leader. Michael Gaismair, who until then was the secretary of the bishop of Brixen, became a commander-in-chief of the insurgents.[146] A council of all the leaders was established with Gaismair as chairman.[147] He must have been between thirty-five and forty years old at the time,[148] was married, and on his way up in the

---

[143] In the description of the basic course of events of the revolt of 1525 in Tyrol I follow mainly the excellent work of Macek and Benedikter. An examination of the primary sources relating to the activities around Brixen, Bozen, and Meran in the main confirmed their work. Additions or corrections are so indicated. For the events around Trent I have depended solely on their work.

[144] *Macek I*, 142-3.

[145] *TLRA, HR* 106. "Es war ein klain ding das kloster zu plundern, Sy wellen die Schlosser vnnd Guggenheuser im Lanndt auch alle Einnemen vnnd dem Fürsten ein freyss Lanndt vberanntwarten Sy wellen auch hin fur nicht mehr Steurn noch Zinsen vnnd souers der Furst nit Zuguet annemen wolt so muess der Furst Auch zum Lanndt hinauss."

[146] A detailed discussion of Gaismair's social and religious views constitutes the heart of this investigation, and therefore only those facts about his life essential for the narration of events will be included here.

[147] *Macek I*, 143-144.

[148] For discussion of Gaismair's age see *Macek I*, 145 note 88 in which an official letter is quoted to the effect that Gaismair was about 34 or 35 years old. Yet elsewhere (TLRA *AFD* II, 56) we read that in August/September 1525 his son carried letters from Sterzing to Gaismair who was then in prison in Innsbruck. If Gaismair was as young as 34 or 35 his son can hardly have been older than 15 which says something for the lad and the quality of the Gaismair home. He was

administrative bureaucracy of the bishopric. An official communication of just over a year later describes Gaismair as follows: "...a lanky, tall, haggard, thin man, about thirty-four or thirty-five years old, wearing a thin black-brown beard, a handsome, small, and pleasant face, close-cropped hair, and walking with a slight stoop. He is highly articulate." [149]

It is certain that the insurgents would not have elected a stranger as their leader, least of all when he was an important member of the hated bishop's staff. Ladurner is therefore likely right in his contention—albeit advanced as evidence of the sinister and unscrupulous nature of the man—that he had long worked in the background, out of sight, through others who were his instruments, until the time came when he could openly assume leadership.[150] While he likely worked *with* others rather than using them as his tools, there can be no doubt that he had participated in the planning for revolt long before the day of his election as leader. That he was able to save the bishop's palace and the convent from destruction, and prevent loss of life among clergy and nobility during the takeover of Brixen on May 10,[151] indicates that the insurgents knew who he was and respected him. In fact, he must have had firm contacts in the outlying areas as well to command the respect and affection he was evidently given by the representatives from the various communities.

His first action was the appropriation of money and goods from New Abbey and the house of the wealthy Cathedral canon Dr. Gregor Angerer for the financial needs of his administration.[152] There seems to be no doubt that, as Macek insists, Gaismair did not appropriate this wealth for himself. It was used primarily to pay his army. The justification for this, although nowhere stated in so many words, was clearly that this wealth had been won from the hard working subjects

---

also old enough to qualify for arrest with his mother and uncles. It may well be, therefore, that he was perhaps as old as 18 and that the officials were out by two or three years in their estimation of Gaismair's age. See also *Macek I*, 353.

[149] Letter of Innsbruck Council to Hans Jakob von Landau, June 13, 1526 printed in Franz, *Der Deutsche Bauernkrieg* II (1935), 338. "...ain langer, aufgeschossner, heger, dunner man, in dem alter ungeferlich 34 oder 35 jar ist, ain swarz praunfarben dunnen part, schons, clains, zimlichs angesicht, ain beschornen kopf und in seinem gang etwas mit dem kopf niderträchtig oder puggelt und vast wol beredt."

[150] Ladurner, *op. cit.*, 86.

[151] Gaismair himself states this in his letter of protest to the government in Innsbruck in the autumn of 1525. Printed by Hollaender in *Der Schlern* 13, 1932, 381.

[152] *Macek I*, 189-190.

of Brixen, and that now it was being returned to them in the form of support for their movement to free themselves from further exploitation. Gaismair's honesty cannot be impugned as has been done by past historians on the basis of the maudlin complaints of Angerer that Gaismair had reduced him to poverty. The wealth that was the product of injustice was now used to restore justice. Gaismair saw himself acting as the agent of God's justice. It is clear that his understanding of God's justice cut across the official doctrines of what constituted God's justice since Emperor and pope, bishop and duke regarded themselves as the custodians of that justice and could base themselves on such venerable teachers as Aquinas and Augustine and numerous papal pronouncements to prove it. Since at least the time of Charlemagne both pope and emperor were regarded as vicars of Christ exercising his authority on earth. When later Gaismair defended himself against charges of theft he stated clearly that he did not accept the charge since it concerned the common good of the people involved in the uprising.[153]

There is also evidence that Gaismair had images removed from New Abbey in 1525.[154] Macek regards this as evidence of Zwinglian influence, since the Zwinglian reformation had adjudged images to be contrary to God's command several years earlier.[155] But the source specifically states that the golden image was removed in order to be sold, the money going to the revolutionary exchequer.[156] The removal of the image was likely motivated at this time as much by economic as by religious considerations.

While we have spoken above about Gaismair's conviction that he was himself destined to restore divine justice to Tyrol, he did not regard his actions as directed against the archduke or the emperor. He was of one mind with the rest of the rebels that their aim was to return a land, purged of the perversion of justice and oppression by prelate and noble, to the sovereign.[157] All his actions during May, June, and July indicate his respect for and reliance on Ferdinand. Gaismair was therefore no anarchist. He saw even the divine Law as enshrined in and administered by human institutions, in this instance the sovereign. He never abandoned that conviction even when the

---

[153] TLRA *Autogramm E 15*.
[154] TLRA *HR 106*, 260.
[155] *Macek III*, 134.
[156] *Macek I*, 188-189, based on *HR 106*, 260.
[157] See note 161 below.

monarchy had given place to a republican order in his Constitution.

This conviction was also given concrete expression in his estimation of his own role. Although he had evidently looked forward to a time when he would assist the triumph of divine justice, he did not step out independently and announce himself as the deliverer. He waited until he was chosen by the people to lead, and then acted always and meticulously in their name. He refused to act in instances where he had no authority from them.[158] He therefore deliberately accepted the controls of the community upon his own thought and action.

The revolutionary council conducted the negotiations with the commissioners of Ferdinand I when they came to Brixen on May 14. Ferdinand had acted with great dispatch and through his commissioners offered amnesty to all insurgents and requested a truce until a Diet could be called where all grievances would be dealt with.[159] But the overall and firm intention of the insurgents had earlier already been agreed upon. They had nothing against the sovereign; their quarrel was with the nobles and the prelates.[160] Gaismair and most of the rebels agreed with the statement made by the peasants in Bozen about this same time: "They had no intention of doing anything improper against his royal highness, their lord and sovereign... [but] not to rest until they returned the castles [of nobles and prelates], and anything else that was mortgaged, to him free and without encumbrance." [161] Leonhard Püchler tried to persuade them to set the condition that Ferdinand would have to agree with their program or else he too would have to go,[162] but was unable to do so.[163]

Their first aim was therefore to return the country to the direct rule of the archduke, for they believed that he would reconfirm their ancient rights and privileges. A further aim of the insurgents was to deprive the clergy of all their secular power. At the beginning of the revolt Bishop Sprentz wrote to Ferdinand that the peasants were firmly determined to exclude all spiritual prelates from secular govern-

---

[158] TLRA *Autogramm E 15.*

[159] Benedikter, *op. cit.*, 78.

[160] *Macek I*, 152.

[161] Quoted by Wopfner, "Bozen im Bauernkrieg von 1525," 180. From ASB, *Cassa 38.* "Sy wern nicht ler maynung ungepurliches wider furstlich durchlaucht... als iren hern und landsfursten fürzunemen ... furter iren kopff nit sanft legen bis furst durchl. ir schlosser und anders, so versetzt, verphendt, frey und ledig überantwurt und zu handen gestelt worden."

[162] The testimony of Lamprecht Schund, AVB, *Rathsprotokoll*, 793.

[163] Benedikter, *op. cit.*, 78.

ment and judiciary power, and to turn it all over to the sovereign.[164] On May 13 the plundering began in Bozen and an uneasy alliance between peasants and townspeople was established.[165] In Sterzing, Lana, and Schlanders the houses of the Teutonic Knights were plundered,[169] everywhere castles fell into the hands of the peasants,[166] and church establishments were plundered in most of the insurgent centres.[168] On May 14 the subjects of Leonhard von Völs, the vice-regent, attacked and seized the fortress of Prösels, partly because of their hate of their lord, but also because the castle held the ancient Rights of the Estates (*Standesprivilegien*).[169] Many nobles simply turned their castles over to the rebels, hoping to save as much as possible.[170]

The result of the royal offer brought to Brixen on May 14 was the calling of a meeting with representatives from all the communities on May 18—Macek calls it a partial Diet (*Teillandtag*)—to determine further action. It is clear that Gaismair and the representatives trusted Ferdinand's word.[171] The offer of amnesty and truce was accepted. No further violence was to take place, but at the same time positions occupied and the gains made by the insurgents were to be left where they were until the grievances could be settled at the projected Diet in Innsbruck.[172] In the meantime the revolutionary council had not been idle. To establish their control and achieve a bargaining position over against clergy and nobility, emissaries were sent to the Salzburg insurgents to plead for solidarity. Appeals for support of the Swiss Confederacy and the Grisons were discussed and probably acted upon. Measures to resist the possible approach of mercenaries were elaborated and the surrender of Rodeneck Castle was called for. A messenger was dispatched to Trent to make contact with the rebels

---

[164] AVB *Urkunde 24626*. Further, bishop of Trent to Ferdinand, July 9, 1525: "daz die geistlichen kain administration in der weltlichait haben" (TLRA *TE*, 135), and the almost verbally identical formulation of Ferdinand to Sprentz on the same date: "dieweil der gemein man in disem land ... darauf verharrt dass die geistlichen kain administration in der weltlichait [haben]" (TLRA, *TE*, 135v).

[165] Benedikter, *op. cit.*, 79-83.

[166] *Ibid.*, 83.

[167] *Ibid.*, 84.

[168] *Macek I*, 159-169.

[169] *Ibid.*, 154.

[170] Benedikter, *op. cit.*, 84.

[171] This is clearly implied in a priestly letter to the Provost of the cathedral of Brixen of July 27, 1525. Gaismair, we read, has remained "treulich in wort auf den fürsten." (ASB, *Cassa 38, 9G*).

[172] *Macek I*, 185-187.

there,[173] and the possibility of seizing the episcopal fortress of Säben above Klausen was considered.[174] After the end of the negotiations Gaismair moved the seat of his administration into the episcopal fortress in Brixen, and proceeded to establish more firmly the power of the revolutionary council.[175]

It is clear that Ferdinand had achieved much by his diplomacy. The truce with its temporary concessions gave him time to overcome his fiscal and military weakness. He exploited the unquestioned confidence of the people in his word cleverly to his own advantage. That he was deliberately deceptive is shown by a letter to Duke Wilhelm of Bavaria in which he stated that he had made a virtue of necessity and had been forced to extend some concessions to the peasants of the Allgäu. Since however he had to negotiate under the threat of force he did not feel obligated to honour his word.[176]

Now the insurgents began to work towards clear and persuasive formulation of their grievances. While Ferdinand was meeting representatives from North Tyrol in Innsbruck and trading some minimal and again temporary concessions for promises to help put down any further insurgency, the news arrived that the peasants of Brixen, Bozen, and Meran had called a Diet in Meran for May 30, excluding nobles and clerics from participation. Ferdinand attempted to prevent the meeting by issuing decrees strictly prohibiting it, but the delegates had left for Meran before the decree arrived. The Diet met from May 30 to June 8, specifically to draw up a list of grievances to be presented to Ferdinand at the general Diet called to meet in Innsbruck in June.

The Meran Articles clearly reveal the concerns of the peasantry.[177] They want nothing less than a new constitution.[178] While the articles are not articulated in biblical language complete with marginal references as was the case with the "Twelve Articles," [179] they nevertheless reveal the same spirit. They speak of the abuses in the social

---

[173] The instruction had broken out there with great force on May 15. (*Ibid.*).

[174] The confession of Lienhart Schnagerer Oct. 18-19, ASB *Cassa 38, 14F* and Sigmund Mair Nov. 3 TLRA *HR* 106, 275v.

[175] Benedikter, *op. cit.*, 91.

[176] *Ibid.*, 92.

[177] *Ibid.*, 93-94.

[178] G. Franz, *Quellen zur Geschichte des Bauernkrieges*, Darmstadt, 1963, 272. It was the first clear step to a movement for a new constitution that stretched back to 1508.

[179] A. Goetze, "Die zwölf Artikel der Bauern 1525," *Historische Vierteljahrschrift* V (1902), 1-33.

body which "hinder the Kingdom of God", a chief one of which is
that men have forgotten to observe love to Christ and goodwill to
the neighbour and that the land's resources have been used selfishly
and not for the common good. The insurrection was a revelation of
divine justice in order to bring back brotherly love and concern for
the common good.[180] There is a clear appeal to the so-called "divine
right", based there on the reformation teaching of the authority of
the Bible, the Word of God, which is to be preached without any
self-seeking additions. That Word speaks of the oneness and equality
of Christian people; no one may enrich himself at the expense of
others. The common good is the norm of action.[181] The first nine
articles deal with the church. It is to be stripped of its worldly power
and its income to go to the sovereign (article 1), the monasteries are
to be gradually dissolved (art. 3, 4, 5) and the hierarchy is to be abolished (art. 2). The church is to be subject to the common law of the land
as everyone else (art. 11). The nobility too is to be deprived of any
special privileges (art. 1, 11, 12). The articles plead for a judiciary
that is elected from among themselves, someone who knows the ways
of the land and the ancient rights (art. 14) and for laws which simplify
and accelerate the judicial process (art. 11, 12). They want to choose
and pay their own pastors, and whatever is left over of the tithe is
to be used for the support of the poor (art. 8). The income from the
secularization of the many benefices and foundations is likewise to
be used in a massive program to help the indigent, especially in the
establishment of hospitals (art. 10). Most of the articles 18-62 deal
with the usual grievances concerning the feudal exactions made by the
landlords,[182] but nowhere is the basic feudal arrangement itself challenged. They demand the removal of the vice-regent Leonhard von
Völs, specifically, and beyond that the total abolition of the office
(art. 14). The rights of the sovereign are in no way infringed by the
articles but rather extended at the expense of clergy and nobility. A
combination of royal power and right and local government is henceforth to be the administration of Tyrol.

A clear understanding of the importance of the Meran articles for
the peasant movement in Tyrol necessitates some comparison with
other peasant grievance submissions. The first and longest of such

---

[180] Franz, *Quellen*, 272.
[181] *Ibid.*, article 3(273), 4(274), 10(274-5), 15(276), 24(278-9), 46(283), 62(285).
[182] See footnotes 10-28.

submissions was that of the Stühlingen peasants.[183] It is clearly distinguished from the Meran articles and other later collections from Swabia in that it makes no appeal to Scripture nor to the divine law. No Reformation influence is noticeable since Reformation teaching had not penetrated to this area.

At the other end of the scale stand the famous Twelve Articles, a kind of distillation of many local grievances, which makes a massive appeal to Scripture, to evangelical teaching, and to divine law. The Meran articles stand somewhere between these two extremes and may be more profitably compared with the Memmingen articles of March, 1525.[184] While both documents detail peasant demands and a return to the divine law, the differences between them are more striking than the resemblances.

First of all, the Meran articles represent the grievances of peasants of the Eisack and Etsch valleys, that is, of a number of communities whereas the Memmingen articles reflect the concerns of one community only. This may in part account for the fact that there are 62 Meran articles but only ten from Memmingen.

The circumstances of authorship of the two documents vary. The author of the Memmingen articles is one man, Sebastian Lotzer.[185] While he was a layman he was biblically and theologically literate. He had published several tracts in which he defended the right of laymen to speak and write about the Word of God.[186] He had been under Zwinglian influence and hence insisted that the Word of God spoke to the practical issues of life.

The Meran articles, on the other hand, have no single author. It seems clear that Michael Gaismair was a leading figure in their formulation, but others participated.[187] While Gaismair too had direct contacts with Zwingli they came only later. At this point in May, 1525, therefore we can posit only indirect and general Reformation influences on the Meran articles in contrast to the Memmingen document which reflects greater proximity to the source of Reformation ideas.

The emphasis on divine law is much stronger in the Memmingen articles than in those from Meran. Moreover they are much more

---

[183] Franz, *Quellen*, 101-123.
[184] *Ibid.*, 168-171; *Bauernkrieg*, 121-122.
[185] Franz, *Bauernkrieg*, 122.
[186] *Ibid.*
[187] See p. 76.

biblically specific. While neither document has direct Scriptural references, the close relationship of the Memmingen articles to the
Twelve Articles, also written by Lotzer, underscores their explicitly
biblical nature.[188] An example of this is the fact that Memmingen
article number two rejects the further payment of the tithe since the
New Testament does not demand it. Meran assumes the continuation of the basic tithe.

[Very noticeable is the much greater militancy of the Meran articles.
They show none of the almost obsequious deference to the authorities
of the Memmingen document. The Memmingen peasants respectfully ask, while the peasants gathered at Meran demand. The Tyrolian
peasants were in a much more truculent mood partly because of their
"successful" revolt, and partly because they were represented in the
Diet where they would shortly lay their demands before the sovereign. They were politically more mature than their Swabian
counterparts.]

[The Meran articles are therefore very much the product of a special
situation reflecting relative remoteness from Reformation influences
and the higher level of political participation and sophistication of
the Tyrolian peasants.]

While this Diet at Meran was in session plans were already being
made for the general Diet to meet in Innsbruck. The preparations
for it had been expertly carried out by Ferdinand with his diplomacy
of divide and conquer and of making temporary concessions which
he had no intention of honouring. For by May 30 the rebel movement in South Tyrol was everywhere, except in Brixen, controlled
by conservative councils in which the towns and the nobility were
represented, which strictly adhered to the agreed truce and thereby
hoped to retain their privileges.[189] Since Ferdinand had been unable
to prevent the Diet of Meran he sent representatives with the instructions to divide, if possible, the honourable estates (*Ehrbarkeit*) from
the *Pofl* (the poor) and so to break the back of the revolt.[190] In fact,
however, the royal officials did not achieve much, if anything, for a
new constitution based on the basic provisions of the Meran Articles
would drastically have changed Tyrolian society, inasmuch as they

---

[188] Franz, *Bauernkrieg*, 123.
[189] *Macek I*, 199-201.
[190] *Ibid.*, 204.

called for a radical reform of the church and for equality before the law of high and low alike.[191]

Because of Ferdinand's fear of the Diet of Meran the date for the general Diet in Innsbruck was moved forward from July 2 to June 12. That gave less time for solidification of the sentiments expressed in the Meran Articles, and earlier opportunity to break the spirit of the revolt and to re-establish ducal authority.

It is clear that Ferdinand called the Diet, not with any intention of seriously dealing with the flood of grievances,[192] but to crush the revolt.[193] He clearly said so in his introductory address on June 12, much to the anger of the delegates. For the peasant delegates were convinced that here at last their ancient grievances would be honestly dealt with. In fact peasant representatives constituted the vast majority of those present, for many of the nobility had not appeared, preferring to remain in the relative safety of their castles, and the clergy were excluded altogether for the worldly power of the church was regarded by the peasants as the chief cause of all their trouble. Also excluded was the hated vice-regent Leonhard von Völs.

Ferdinand had surrounded himself with whatever support he could get. First of all he favoured and got the support of the nobility. There were representatives from the Swabian League, sworn enemies of the peasants, as also from the Dukes of Bavaria. On the other side were the peasants who fell into two groups; the well-to-do, who constituted the majority of the delegates, and who, while they wanted their demands met, were anxious to accomplish their goal by negotiation, and the delegates from Brixen and Trent who represented the poorer people, were much more radical, and therefore not as ready for compromises.

Ferdinand was without money and without arms and was thus unable to force his will on the stubborn peasants. He therefore resorted to deceptive diplomacy to gain time until he conld follow the example of the Swabian League. In his opening address on June 12 he told the lie that he was only governor of Tyrol for Charles V his brother, and that therefore he had only limited powers to act upon peasant de-

---

[191] *Macek I*, 204, 208, 211, 217, gives Ferdinand's representatives too much credit for aiding in conservatizing the articles. The basic ingredient, the veneration of Ferdinand and the implicit trust in his word, were already there.

[192] All of these are printed in Wopfner, *Quellen zur Geschichte des Bauernkrieges in Deutschtirol.*

[193] *Macek I*, 196, footnote 70, and 221. For detailed description and analysis of the Diet see *Macek I*, 221-290 and Benedikter *op. cit.*, 96-106.

mands.[194] Although the radicals, especially Leonhard Püchler, openly charged that Ferdinand was lying, most of the delegates continued in their confidence in the goodwill of the sovereign. Ferdinand was thus able to use his lie to considerable advantage.

The delegates decided to conduct the deliberations on the basis of the Meran Articles. Moreover they agreed that the discussions were to be carried on in plenary session rather than in committee, and that they would vote by individual delegate rather than by representation in committee. That gave the peasant delegation virtual control of the Diet. But on June 14 came the news that the Swabian League had destroyed a peasant army of 15,000 at Würzburg. That same day the nobles were admitted to the Diet as full participants, and by June 16 business was again conducted in committee. The already conservative tendencies of many farm and town delegates, the news from Würzburg and Ferdinand's diplomacy that divided the peasant delegation and encouraged the well-to-do deal with the nobles, directed the Diet into quieter waters. By June 20 many of the radical delegates had left, convinced that their cause had been betrayed and that nothing could be expected from the Diet. On June 22 the Innsbruck Articles were read. These were actually the Meran Articles to which 32 others were added to include grievances from areas not represented at Meran. Five days later Ferdinand replied, pleading again that he had only gubernatorial powers and that he could not change the constitution. Moreover he defended the clergy and the nobles by saying that everything that had been taken from them during the early days of the revolt would have to be returned. On June 30 the delegates replied to Ferdinand's response. They now said they had no intention of forcing a new constitution; they merely wanted their grievances dealt with. But although the peasant delegates continued to commit themselves to the Meran Articles, the nobles, now full participants, obviously could not. Compromises had to be reached and the prospect for the basic changes called for at Meran began to fade.

Ferdinand also began to see a way to disarm the chief centre of revolt. The Meran Articles demanded that the secular power of the church be handed over to the sovereign. If now he agreed to this point temporarily in some measure, it would appear like a major concession. Thus, along with some minor concessions he consented on July 3 to assume control of the prince-bishopric of Brixen and thereby

---

[194] This is a fact, clearly demonstrated by the sources. See *Macek I*, 239-240, 151 note 116.

deprived Gaismair and the revolutionary council of its power at one stroke. But for this favour he demanded and got the cooperation of all the delegates for the suppression of the revolt. The delegates continued to trust Ferdinand, rejoicing that at least one of the big prelates and his prerogatives had forever gone. No one would have believed that this secularization was a sham and would in fact last only a few months. On July 9 Ferdinand sent his commissioners to Brixen to negotiate the surrender of power with Gaismair.

Ferdinand's final words to the Diet were spoken on July 18. The revolt was to be put down—they had agreed to that and he thanked them. The details of the procedure were to be put in writing. The confiscated property of those punished was to be divided three ways: one-third to the sovereign, one-third to him who carried out the penalty, and one-third to the informer. A permanent committee of twelve representing the estates was to rework the Innsbruck Articles into a new constitution. But that would take time, and that is what Ferdinand needed most, second only to money.

Actually it is clear that the peasants gained considerable relief, temporarily, although most of the gains went to those who were already well-to-do. Still, the cures of the Innsbruck Diet dealt only with symptoms. Virtually nothing was left of the high expectations of the Meran Articles dealing with the equality of man and the "divine law". And even the gains referred to above were swept away again when the constitution of 1526, which came out of the Diet of Innsbruck, was suspended in 1532. Ferdinand had never intended to make it permanent.

Meanwhile Michael Gaismair and the revolutionary council back in Brixen meticulously observed the truce and had kept strict order in dependence on Ferdinand's word. Nevertheless they continued to strengthen their military potential which probably reflects Gaismair's uneasiness at the news from Innsbruck and his determination to see through his plan to deprive the church of its secular power. His conconcern and uneasiness are also reflected in his letter to his former employer Bishop Sprentz which he wrote on June 19.[195] It is first of

---

[195] See English translation in Appendix pp. 123-124. Macek's footnote on p. 243 of *Der Tiroler Bauernkrieg* is confusing. He states that he was unable to find the original which Hollaender used for his publication in *Der Schlern* 13, 1932 in Bolzano. The original is in fact in the TLRA in Innsbruck in the package of documents registered under *Hofregistratur* A IV 30, 106, along with a photocopy. The copy which Hollaender used in Bolzano was turned over to the "Reichsgauarchiv" (TLRA) in October, 1943 by the Gauleiter, presumably because the

all necessary to decide what prompted this letter signed "Your submissive Michel Gaismair." The letter itself supplies the chief clue.
Towards the end of the letter Gaismair writes that it would have
been impossible for one man to have started and carried out a revolt
in three days over the whole country without extensive advance pre-
paration. That suggests that Gaismair is here defending himself
against the evidently widespread official view that he himself was
responsible for the revolt.[196] He is making his defence to the bishop as
the man he knows best, hoping perhaps that a residue of the former
trusting relationship between them is still left and that the bishop is
the most likely person to believe him. He had firmly believed until
now that the peasant grievances would be dealt with and satisfied at
the Diet. He stood for a peaceful legal settlement, and he is anxious
not to have that possibility destroyed by false rumours.

It is in this context that we should see Gaismair's description in
this letter of his own role in the May revolt. In the first place, he
writes, the revolt began before he was chosen as leader, and when he
joined it he exercised a restraining influence. He saved the bishop's
palace from plunder and himself took of the bishop's means only
what he needed for the upkeep of the soldiers needed to preserve order
and peace according to the terms of the truce arranged earlier with
Frederick's officials. All of that rests on fact and is not a misrepresentation as Macek asserts. There is no doubt that Gaismair's leadership
brought discipline and order to the revolutionary movement and in
this way, certainly, slowed down its momentum.

The letter is at the same time an attempt to explain his own actions to his former employer. Here we find the only instance that could
be regarded as an exaggeration or misrepresentation, namely his claim
that he took upon himself the leadership of the revolt at great cost
to himself and his family only to serve the bishop's interests. It may
even be that his explanation is evidence of a measure of uncertainty
on Gaismair's part because of the ambiguous situation in which he
found himself as a result of the developments at the Diet in Innsbruck. He no doubt remembered the terrible justice of the bishop

Nazis showed considerable interest in Gaismair. According to Hans Benedikter
in an oral communication there were plans to make a film on Gaismair in 1943,
and it may be that the autograph was brought to Innsbruck in that connection.
Thus the document which Macek used in the TLRA was evidently the autograph
for which he looked in vain in L'Archivio di Stato Bolzano!

[196] That this was the case can be seen unambiguously from the subsequent
procedure of Innsbruck against Gaismair.

against his subjects in April, and the possibility that he too might experience that justice. His request to burn the letter lest it be used against him by his fellow rebels is also intelligible on this interpretation. It is not a betrayal of the revolution on Gaismair's part but it could easily be misunderstood as such. Gaismair's faith in Ferdinand was still intact at this time, but some members of the revolutionary council did not share his confidence. Any individual peace feeler with the hated bishop would be misconstrued by them. Finally, the submissive address and signature is no evidence of attempt to demonstrate loyalty nor a sign of obsequiousness. It is simply part of the formality of address customary in those circumstances. Gaismair used the same terms in his letter of October 9/10 to the royal Council (*Hofrat*), a document not generally characterized by submissiveness.[197]

The letter is not even a contradiction of Gaismair's intention to deprive the clergy of their secular power. It was suggested above that Gaismair considered himself called by God to bring divine justice to victory. That same idea occurs again in this letter. He writes: "In my estimation [the revolt] is a work of God and not of man. For no man in his own power could have produced such an event throughout the whole land in three days without any conspiracy or consultation." [198] He may have had in mind here firstly the fact that he was not with the rebels on May 9-12, and that therefore he could on that ground alone not be held solely responsible. His main argument, however, is that this event was brought about by God, that he was caught up in it, and could have done nothing to prevent it even if he had had a mind to try. He now hopes that God will himself establish "a Christian peace, law, and constitution," for since God began this revolt, he will also bring it to its conclusion with a new just order. There is therefore every reason to assume that Gaismair planned to continue in his role and he hopes the bishop will now understand what has happened in Brixen and to him as bishop. Gaismair then

---

[197] Macek's explanation for the letter to Sprentz in I, 243-244 cannot account for Gaismair's revolutionary actions of calling in radical clergy at precisely the time he was writing the letter. Benedikter's judgement that it was a deliberate attempt to deceive the bishop just does not agree with the tone of the letter. In any event, Gaismair will have known that such an attempt was useless since the bishop had his informers in Brixen and therefore knew the true state of affairs.

[198] Hollaender, *Der Schlern* 13, 1932, 378-379. "... dann meines achtens so ist das ain werckh gotes und kainer menschen. Aus dem ann ainiche praticken oder beratschlagung in dreyen tagen ain solhe tatt durch das gantz land beschehen ist, das kainem menschen aus aigener macht zu tun nit wol muglich sein mag."

admonishes the bishop to commit himself to God for God does not forsake his own.[199]

An attempt was made above to demonstrate that the central biblical emphasis on justice, mercy, and humility was an important stimulant to action for Gaismair. On June 21, 1525, it was reported that Gaismair had brought an evangelical preacher to Brixen,[200] an action which coincided with his letter to Sprentz. This is the first clear indication of Gaismair's movement away from Catholicism towards some form of evangelical religion. The churches had been closed in Brixen since June 1. Thus it is likely that Gaismair had in mind to provide the people with religious guidance now that the old church had been deprived of its place as teacher. This indicates that religious issues were matters of primary importance to Gaismair and that he thought in terms of some organized religious activity. Who this cleric was or where he came from is not known, but it is certain that he shared Gaismair's views, for on July 29 the Council wrote to Anton Brandisser, the interim administrator of the prince-bishopric, that the man was preaching overthrow and rebellion.[201] It is also certain that he was no Lutheran. It may therefore be that the man was an adherent of Zwingli for Zwingli had written strongly in 1523 about the legitimacy of deposing evil rulers who oppress the people.[202] This calling of a preacher to whom others were soon added [203] testifies again to Gaismair's conviction that the social and religious are by no means separated. He saw his action as part of God's work to liberate the people from physical and spiritual bondage. He evidently chose men who were not easily frightened, for instructions came out of Innsbruck, with great regularity, to stop them until long after Gaismair was no longer in Tyrol. They were clearly also men who gained the affection and support of the people.[204] This is evidence that Gaismair had taken

---

[199] From this perspective Gaismair's words are very reminiscent of a passage in the *Reformatio Sigismundi* when the author writes that the clergy would be quite secure even without their secular power (Koller, *op. cit.*, 232).

[200] *Macek I*, 245.

[201] TLRA *TE*, 160.

[202] "Auslegen und Gründe der Schlussreden," *ZSW* II, 346 (Art. 42). A letter of the Council to the magistrate in Sterzing on Jan. 7, 1526 speaks specifically about a Zwinglian cleric (TLRA *TE*, 475v).

[203] TLRA *TE*, 353-354. (Letter of Council to Brandisser, Oct. 4, 1525); 463v-464 (Letter of Council to the administrator of the house of the Teutonic Knights, Dec. 23, 1525); *AFD* II, 82-84 (Dec. 28, 1525).

[204] TLRA *TE*, 208v, 236, 272. All of these communications reflect the difficulty of proceeding against the dissident clerics because of the support which they enjoyed among the people.

pains to carry out his plans for change responsibly and effectively, a clear indication of how seriously he took his Christian convictions. It would be going too far, however, to speak of Gaismair as a Zwinglian Protestant at this point. Nevertheless his developing convictions were such that a move in that direction would not be unexpected. Perhaps the expectation of aid from Zürich had something to do with his theological sympathies.

4. The Radicalizing of Gaismair August, 1525 to January, 1526

Because of the news brought back by delegates from the Brixen area that things were not going well for the revolutionaries at the Diet, Gaismair himself went to Innsbruck apparently hoping he could avert disaster.[205] By now he was evidently no longer certain about the goodwill of Ferdinand, and his visit to Innsbruck may have convinced him that he had been leaning on a pointed staff. Nevertheless he was determined to adhere to the truce. Before he left he told his friends: "Keep quiet and don't start a new uprising here. The peace will not last; the trouble will begin again at Schwaz and other places. But we must not be the ones to start it again, for I am very reluctant to cause more bloodshed." [206] At the same time he was also prepared for further action, perhaps of a non-military nature, by putting the Archduke under economic pressure by paralyzing the customs collection in the south. Under such pressure he would have to listen to them and they would be able to gain their ends.[207] This reveals that he now saw himself as resisting not merely the nobles and prelates but also Ferdinand.

Gaismair and his Council recognized the action of Ferdinand for what it was and resisted the transfer of authority. These events began on July 10 when Ferdinand's officials came to Brixen to prepare for the takeover. Gaismair evidently publicly stated his opposition to

---

[205] *Macek I*, 268.

[206] *ASB, Cassa 38*, 14 F. (Confession of Hans Kastner). "Stet still vnd macht khain auffruer hie, wan die sachen wurden nit pleyben. Es wurd mal zu Swaz und ander orten wider auffgeen dz wir alhier nit die sein so die auffrur machen dan ich wollt nit gern dz plut vergiessen pescheen sollt."

[207] This is based on the following sentence of the preceding quotation. "Und wan man die posteien vnd confinen ins land pesturzt so macht vns der fursst nit widerstand thun . . ." What this means is not quite clear, but Macek's assumption that it refers to an occupation of the border fortresses is not satisfactory. One should also not forget that Gaismair's words are being reported by someone else.

surrendering power and also that he had plans that went much further than those of some of his associates.[208] In fact he seems almost to have lost his head when he finally saw through Ferdinand's duplicity. It must have been about this time that he uttered threats against the Archduke. Hans Kastner reported Gaismair as saying that if he became convinced that the sovereign threatened him he would disguise himself and put a bullet through him.[209] These words may have emerged from an acute sense of betrayal; he had implicitly trusted Ferdinand and scrupulously conducted himself accordingly. His frustration was heightened by the fact that he knew himself to be responsible to and for many others who would now suffer because of his misplaced trust. It is also possible that regular contact and discussion with the preachers he had brought in had first suggested to him the possibility of tyrannicide. Evidently he connected Ferdinand's actions with the machinations of the prelates, a conclusion not without its justification.[210] Thus he was heard to say that "things would never improve until all the clerics were killed." [211] Now he also threatened to provoke a full-scale revolt.[212]

The events of the summer but especially the double play of Ferdinand had forced Gaismair into a more radical position than he had earlier held. This was undoubtedly nourished by the influence of the radical clerics. Their activities and views are described in a letter of Ferdinand to the Council on December 20, 1525. These men preach "against God, his saints, and the venerable christian rites of the church ... also against the spiritual and worldly authority ... Some persons are saying impermissible things against our own person, our government and counsellors, through which the common man is

---

[208] Letter of Johann Kauttinger to the Dean of the Cathedral, July 27, 1525, *ASB Cassa 38*, 9, IG. The letter states that Gaismair had conducted himself "treulich in wort auf den fürsten." But now, "Ich glaub auch, daz er daz sloss nit werd absteen, wan er hat ain besundern verstand, mer dann jemand so sich haben rebellirt als offentlich hie die reden umbgeen."

[209] TLRA *AFD*, II, 49f. "... der Cosster [Kastner] bekennt daz Michel Gaismair Ee Er hieher komen ist geredt hab wo Er wisste daz Im E. f. D. drolich were so wolt Er E. f. D. enntleiben oder ain Kugel in sy schiessen vnd sich zu solichen sunnderlich verclaiden." See also *ASB Cassa 38*, 14, F.

[210] Ferdinand had been in touch with the prelates all along and he sympathized with Angerer's attempt to get back the property he claimed Gaismair had stolen from him.

[211] ASB *Cassa 38*, 14 F. Confession of Hans Kastner. "Es thu khain guet man schlag dan die pfaffen alle zu tod."

[212] *Ibid.*, "Er wollt auch ain land pewegen vnd an sich hengen."

provoked to rebellion and disobedience to us, his authority." [213] It is probable that Gaismair shared these views. If that is so, then he had now moved further away from Catholicism into a rejection of the church's claims to spiritual authority and the rites of the church, presumably chiefly the Mass as the central religious observance of the church. At Zürich the Mass had been declared to be erroneous in October, 1523, on theological grounds.[214] One of the preachers Gaismair brought into Tyrol had settled at Sterzing.[215] This man is likely identical with the preacher named Hans Vischer referred to in a communication to the Council April 27, 1526.[216] He is also likely the same one referred to in a letter of the Council to Ferdinand on June 14, 1526, where it is stated that he had left and gone to a disputation at Baden in the Aargau.[217] It was presumably the disputation that took place in the town in May, 1526 between Catholics and Zwinglians. This strongly suggests that this preacher was a Zwinglian, which in turn strengthens the supposition that Gaismair was gradually drawn towards the Zwinglian brand of Protestantism. This Hans Vischer expressed himself on the Mass but only to say that it was superstitious magic. While this is not a theological explanation for the error of the Mass it is a rejection of its sacramental value which was characteristic of the Zwinglian position. Vischer also rejected extreme unction as being no more than "a snap of the fingers".

Again, both in Ferdinand's description of the teachings of the radical preachers, as also in the views of Hans Vischer, we have the combination of religious and social radicalism. While both of these reports are dated some months after July, 1525, we may justifiably assume that this broad statement was representative of their earlier views as well. That the authorities complained about their subversive preaching we have already seen. We therefore conclude that Gaismair's religious and social views at this point reflect increasingly a Zwinglian

---

[213] TLRA *VKM* I, 278f. "... wider Got, sein heiligen vnd die löblichen cristenlichen gebrauch der Kirchen, sonndern auch wider die geistlich vnd weltlich obrigkait predigen ... auch durch sonnder personen wider vnser aigen person Regierungen vnd Rät vil vngeschickt Reden gebraucht werden sollen dardurch der gemain man zu widerwillen geraizt wirdet vnnd sich gegen vnns seiner oberkait abwuerfft vnd ungehorsam macht ...."

[214] "Die Akten der zweiten Disputation vom 26-28. Oktober 1523", *ZSW* II, 664-803.

[215] See note 203 above.

[216] TLRA *TE*, 597.

[217] TLRA *AFD* II, 289v.

position, but we lack any specific evidence attributing these views to him.

The pressure to modify the revolutionary demands which was so obvious at the Innsbruck Diet was being felt in Brixen as well. The well-to-do wanted no further unrest and pressed for surrender, adopting a hostile stance toward the *Pofl*. Gaismair soon saw that it was futile to resist the sovereign and the decision of the wealthy and the nobility and reluctantly yielded. On July 21 Ferdinand issued a decree demanding loyalty and obedience from all subjects of the prince-bishopric, and at the end of July the transferral of authority took place with detailed accounting of his administration by Gaismair.

If Ferdinand thought that his victory at the Diet had crushed the revolt he was mistaken. The radicals continued to meet to decide on further action. But more importantly, there was widespread resistance to the acceptance of the decisions of the Diet,[218] and many subjects around Brixen refused to pay the customary dues to Ferdinand's representatives. The preacher whom Gaismair had brought to Brixen continued his efforts to rouse the peasants to new resistance in spite of attempts to arrest him.[219] Gaismair himself went to Bozen and Sterzing to gather support against the decisions of the Diet but was unsuccessful since many there had lost all heart for further open resistance.

On August 11 Gaismair received an invitation to appear in Innsbruck ostensibly to discuss the unrest which had followed upon the transfer of power.[220] With reluctance and some suspicion he left on August 20, and on his arrival in Innsbruck found his suspicions fully justified for he was forthwith unceremoniously imprisoned. With this action the Innsbruck officials removed a major hindrance to the final pacification of the country since Gaismair was no longer there to unify centres of discord for renewed resistance. That Ferdinand had no intention of honourable discussion with Gaismair is shown by a letter to Karl Trapp, one of the nobles responsible for punishing the insurgents, in which on August 18, two days before Gaismair's departure, Ferdinand requested any information which could be used in the

---

[218] The codex *Tiroler Empörung* clearly reveals the widespread disillusionment about the results of the Diet. The following references with dates are some of the instances of resistance. 193 (Aug. 17), 196 (Aug. 17), 198v (Aug. 18), 201 (August 18), 201v (Aug. 18), 205v-206 (Aug 20), 213-213v (Aug. 23), 214 (Aug. 23), 227-227v (Aug. 27), 236v (Aug. 29), 247v (Aug. 31).

[219] TLRA *TE* 160, 202.

[220] *Ibid.*, 180.

proceedings against Gaismair.[221] The royal Council now extracted an oath from Gaismair that he would not leave Innsbruck without their permission.[222] On September 26 they got information from Wilhelm Liechtenstein that Gaismair had indeed spoken out against the decisions of the Diet. They therefore could now proceed against him.[223] To satisfy the unceasing complaints of Dr. Gregor Angerer, a high cleric from Brixen, that Gaismair had robbed him of valuables, Gaismair's property was ordered confiscated on September 27, leaving only enough for the family to live on.[224] In the meantime the revolutionary preachers were busy in Sterzing, Meran and Brixen, preaching openly against the decisions of the Diet, and Innsbruck was reluctant to prosecute because of the dangerous mood among the people. The strongest penalty recommended was exile.[225]

The revolt had again flared up in Trent in the beginning of July but had been put down by the end of August, due to inexperience, lack of unity among the farmers, and the inability to link arms with Brixen. But now Ferdinand was ready. His time had been well used since May. Now, because of a successful loan granted by the nobles and prelates of Tyrol and the Fuggers of Augsburg, he also had money, and that meant that he could finally hire mercenaries to pacify the land. On September 7, two thousand mounted men rode out of Innsbruck to make peace in the land. Together with the rack and assorted other tortures as well as the executioner, justice was administered. The bishop of Trent contributed liberally to the agony of his subjects. Everywhere terrible, bloody retribution was meted out, prevailing legal provisions regarding right to trial also becoming victims of the pacification. Everywhere the people submitted now, although a deep resentment continued to glow beneath the surface. Many chose to flee rather than submit to Habsburg justice and went to Venice, long an enemy of the Habsburgs.

While Gaismair was in prison he had frequent visitors, evidently unknown to the authorities, among them his brother Hans and his wife Magdalena. Another relative, Wolf Gaismair came to Innsbruck

---

[221] *Ibid.*, 200. Similar letters were written to others on Sept. 20, *Ibid.*, 313 and 315v, and on Sept. 26, 331.

[222] *Ibid.*, 212.

[223] *Ibid.*, 330v.

[224] *Ibid*, 337.

[225] *Ibid.*, 160 (July 29), 202 (Aug. 19), 208v (Aug. 21), 236 (Aug. 29), 272 (Sept. 6), 332v (Sept. 26), 353-354 (Oct. 4), 337v (Oct. 17), 379 (Oct. 18).

with a loaded gun, perhaps in the hope of setting the prisoner free. Gaismair's own son carried letters back and forth.[226]

It was probably the news of the confiscation of his property and the jeopardy in which this placed the family that prompted Gaismair to escape on the night of October 7.[227] The Council was in a panic and feverishly sent letters in all directions with warnings that the dangerous man was at large.[228] He was now presented as the chief rebel, without honour because he had broken his oath. What was not said was that according to prevailing law he should have been brought to trial within two weeks of his incarceration. He had spent seven weeks there. Suspecting that he had gone back to Sterzing, Gaismair's wife and son, his brother Hans, and others were immediately arrested and threatened with torture if they did not betray him.

Instructions from Innsbruck about questioning them show that by October 12 Gaismair's written protest against the injustice done him and his family, especially his wife, had been received.[229] In the first section he again describes the nature of his actions during the uprising in Brixen. His argument that he contributed to peace and order both before and after he was chosen as leader we have already met in his letter to Sprentz and varies from that only in details. The intention here too is to show that rather than be charged with causing the revolt he should be rewarded for preventing a worse disaster. His insistence that he did not cause the revolt is, in fact, somewhat legalistic if we grant that he had worked in secret for just such an event. The letter reveals an angry man, his acute sense of justice outraged, stating the legal case for his departure, and requesting safe conduct to a legal hearing of the charges against him. He protests that his treatment at the hands of the Council is complete disregard for the ancient law of the land, the amnesty proclaimed by Ferdinand in May, and the decisions of the recent Diet. Thus he is, even at this time apparently, entertaining no thoughts such as those expressed later in his Constitution, that is, the complete overthrow of the prevailing system. His massive appeal to existing law shows that clearly enough. He is protesting therefore not against the prevailing system but against the arbitrariness of those who held the power of adminis-

---

[226] *Ibid.*, 366v-367v.

[227] See Appendix I, p. 127.

[228] *Ibid.*, 358-360v.

[229] *Ibid.*, 366v-367v. The letter printed by Hollaender, "Michel Gaismair's Landesordnung 1526," *Der Schlern* 13, 381-383. See Appendix I pp. 124-129 for English translation.

tering it. He is especially outraged that he does not have access to justice equal to that of the powerful and wealthy prelates Angerer and Gräfinger, against whom much of this protest is directed. They have resources and power to get what they claim as their right, even to the point of pressuring the Council to act contrary to the law, while he has had no opportunity, in spite of requests, to act in his own defence by getting witnesses. He had not had the means for legal counsel, and had received no reply to a request for guarantee of his own safety at a trial, presumably against the murderous wrath of the prelates.

He does not claim to be perfect—a veiled acknowledgement that charges could be brought against him based on the law of the land. He asks for understanding, however, that he had to act in consideration of the people he was with, but always with an eye to keeping the peace. What he took he used for the preservation of order, the same argument he used in the letter to Sprentz. These factors, he suggests, ought to be weighed against each other, and the situation seen in its totality in order for a just assessment to follow. Gaismair knew that even if a man was guilty—and he must have known they could construct a case against him—he had the right to a fair trial according to the law.

It could be suggested that his complaint that Angerer and the Council had acted contrary to the decisions of the Diet was disqualified by his own actions against it. In fact, it was not. What the Diet had decided, as he specifically states, was to proceed henceforth not on the basis of written (Roman) law, but on the basis of the common law of the land.[230] His action against the decisions of the Diet was not a rejection of the above-mentioned decision. Rather it was motivated by the fact that in the end the power and privilege of the well-to-do was confirmed while the poor were sent away empty. They had received some concessions, but the power of administering justice remained, as before, in the hands of the feudal lord. At that level nothing had changed and Gaismair knew that arbitrariness in the administration of justice would continue. Ferdinand had achieved his expressed aim, namely to use the Diet to suppress the movement for greater and more equal justice. Gaismair had wanted to insure that

---

[230] "... dan wiewol in diesem jungst gehalten lanndtag clärlich beschlossen, das nun hinfuro in land nicht nach den geschribnen rechten, sonnder nach dem lanndsprauch, den auch f. dt. vormals confirmirt und menigklich darbei zu hanndthaben zuegesagt hat procedirt werden sol."

the poor and powerless would have some continuing way of achieving redress. That had not happened; hence his opposition, perhaps in the hope that such opposition might still avail to gain what he desired, but certainly on the ground that in his estimation the purpose of the Diet had been subverted. Gaismair's distinction between the law itself and the people and process involved in its execution could not possibly find acceptance by the feudal lords, for they considered the law to be there for the preservation of their privilege, and since they held the power of administration, they could, and did, pervert it to their benefit.

Gaismair now leaves no doubt in the reader's mind that unless the actions against him were discontinued and his request for justice granted, he would move to open rebellion. Eighteen communities along the Eisack will come to his defence as soon as he asks for it, for the "embers are still glowing." He would very much like to avoid any further rebellion but will not be responsible for such an event should justice not be given.

The chief targets of his threats are, in his words, "the godless monks and priests." Godlessness in this instance means the irresponsible and repressive use of power and the bearing of false witness. In particular Gaismair means the violence which the prelates have used against his family and friends. Godlessness therefore has, in Gaismair's view, little to do with the then current conception of godlessness, namely conscious and wilful resistance of the sacral claims of church and secular authority. Gaismair's view of godlessness is that of Jesus and the prophets, namely that it is the heartless and unconscionable exploitation of those who cannot defend themselves. One may perhaps also be permitted to reverse that and say that therefore Gaismair's view of what it meant to be godly was not, as in the contemporary definition, orthodox belief, but just and merciful conduct. A man who is unjust and unmerciful to the poor is therefore godless even if he is a sacramentally ordained clergyman.

A special point should be made of Gaismair's defence of his wife in this letter. As Macek rightly points out, such a defence is extremely rare in the sixteenth century.[231] Here too Gaismair had evidently broken through the prevailing dogmas, for his defence is unintelligible if he shared the view of his contemporaries regarding women.

[231] *Macek I*, 356. Cf. Beda Weber's comment on Gaismair's wife as "half masculine and vain," (*Die Stadt Bozen*, 78).

The prevailing estimate of woman at that time, dominated as it was by a masculine church with its emphasis on celibacy, was that virtue was the prerogative of the male, and that woman was the source of all vice, especially of vanity. She was therefore not to be commended but rather disciplined, not to be defended but chastised.[232] For Gaismair however, his wife was a person of value and respect, equal to himself. She was not just an appendage to him that could be used like a thing to incriminate him. Both she and the infant she was nursing deserved full respect accorded honourable persons, and no one had any right to threaten or frighten them.

This letter therefore confirms the conclusions reached about Gaismair's views above. It is a persuasive expression of Gaismair's strong sense of justice based on the divine law that all men are equal and that they have equal right to justice. Any oppressor puts himself in opposition to God, even if he is a priest. Stronger than before he reveals his conviction that if the present executors of divine justice default in their duty, others will openly dispute their right to rule. The consciousness of his own role in this process is unmistakable. Unless justice is done he will give the signal, reluctantly, to challenge again the holders of power. At the same time the whole letter is a tribute to his continuing efforts to work for justice and equality short of armed rebellion. He was patient and quite prepared, even at this time, to go the second mile with the authorities in Innsbruck.

The fact that the letter was received in Innsbruck within five days of Gaismair's escape indicates the heat of his indignation as well as his sense of urgency about his justification. Hourly the net was being drawn more and more tightly around him. Any time he might be apprehended again, for the decree of October 7 calling for his recapture was known and acted upon throughout Tyrol. The Council wrote to Ferdinand on October 17 that Gaismair should be granted the safe-conduct since he had evidently asked for it in the hope that it would be refused. It would be easy to arrest him again at the point the safe-conduct became invalid.[233] The same day the magistrate at Sterzing received orders to release Gaismair's relatives but to have them secretly watched in case they should contact him.[234] Ferdinand agreed to the suggestion of his Council regarding the safe-conduct

---

[232] Norbert Hölzl, "Tirols Landesfurst als Komödischreiber," *Tiroler Tageszeitung*, Apr. 10, 1971, 15.
[233] TLRA *AFD* II, 56-57.
[234] TLRA *TE*, 378, 386v.

and the proposed arrest.[235] They were, however, in no hurry to publish the safe-conduct for they still hoped to capture him.

But by this time Gaismair was no longer in the country. In fact he must have left immediately after writing his protest, for a communication from Jacob Trapp, royal administrator (*Pfleger*) in Glurns of December 9, 1525, relates that Gaismair passed through Schluderns and Taufers on his way to Switzerland on the Sunday before St. Gall's Day (October 16).[236] He was evidently intent on getting out of the way of the government agents as quickly as possible, and on making contact with Zwingli in Zürich.

The report of his flight through Schluderns and Taufers in the upper Vintschgau also includes something Gaismair told his travelling companions once when they were safely inside the Grisons. He had gunsmiths, he is reported to have said, and he would take down all the church bells and make guns out of them. Then he would show the rulers a thing or two.[237] He had thus by this time firmly resolved to foment a new rebellion against the rulers in Tyrol. It was this resolve that prompted his immediate departure for Zürich with several members of his clan and several men from the Engadine,[238] to consult with Zwingli, an outspoken opponent of the Habsburgs and their policies. Gaismair had therefore concluded that his confidence in Ferdinand and the Council in Innsbruck had been misplaced and that he would now begin to carry out the threat made in his protest. His contacts with Zwingli were to influence him decisively.

It was from Zürich that he sent a second letter to the Council dealing with the same issues on October 25.[239] It may be that he merely

---

[235] TLRA *VKM* I, 256.

[236] TLRA *HR* 106, 240. This represents a more precise dating than found in Macek's *Der Tiroler Bauernkrieg*, 358, and locates Gaismair in the Grisons at least three weeks earlier.

[237] TLRA *HR 106*, 240.

[238] *Ibid.*

[239] TLRA *Autogramm E 15*. See English translation in Appendix I pp. 129-131. For some reason Macek omits any mention of this letter in his work. Benedikter mentions it in *op. cit.*, 127 in one sentence. This is doubly strange since in the story of Gaismair any written witness of the subject himself is important since there are so few. Moreover it represents an important line in the sequence of events and in the development of Gaismair's attitude to the constituted authority of Tyrol. The nineteenth century copy of the original in *Bibliotheca Tirolensis Ferdinandei (Dipauliana) (BTFD) Codex 1082*, 7-8v, and Hoffmann's copy of the copy in *op. cit.* App. IV, both contain major sense-disturbing errors. The letter was delivered in Innsbruck on Nov. 14 as is indicated on the outside of the original letter. The unusually long time taken to deliver the letter is further evidence that Gaismair was no longer in Sterzing and supports the conclusion that

wanted to expand on the earlier protest since he adduces several new
legal points to strengthen his case. But these very points also drove
him further from his earlier offer to appear for judgement. He re-
marks that he has received no reply to his earlier letter. About the
charges of Dr. Angerer he writes that these concern all those involved
in the revolt and they have given him no instructions to act for them
in the matter. He refuses therefore to submit to judgement on the
issue by himself. Secondly and more significantly, the matter of re-
imbursement for losses is a concern of the whole country. It is wellknown, he writes, that Ferdinand granted amnesty to all participants, and the Diet made no decisions about reparations. No town or
jurisdiction gave its representatives or the executive committee any
instructions or authority to act in this matter. It is clear, however,
what is happening. Once Ferdinand left the country and the Diet was
dissolved, Ferdinand's counsellors and the nobility, making common
cause, are taking it upon themselves to demand reparations. This
represents a grave wrong against the land; first of all because they
have not been given the right and secondly, because they have a
vested interest in it. If they call for reparations for Dr. Angerer then
they will call for reparations for themselves too, since some of them
also suffered losses. Judges who stand to gain financially from their
judgements are properly under suspicion of judging wrongly and
therefore he will not submit to their judgement. Even if that were not
the case, he continues, he has no access to an advocate so that he and
his family and friends could even get justice let alone advantage.
Thus he is not obligated to appear for judgement without all the
others involved. Nor are the Council and the Committee authorized
to give judgement in the absence of the sovereign and the representatives of the people. And should such judgement be given in the absence of all those legally required to be there, he will in no way be
bound by it.

Again we find a powerful concern for justice. He implies that he is
not ashamed to submit himself to an impartial court and that he does

---

he was already in Zürich. The first intimation the government had of Gaismair's
whereabouts comes on Nov. 8 in the report of a spy (see note 251 below) which
locates him in Fideris in the Grisons. This was acknowledged officially in a letter
of Nov. 23, 1525 (Macek mistakenly cites Nov. 13 following Schadelbauer) from
Ferdinand to the Zürich Council (Staatsarchiv Zürich, *Beziehungen zum Ausland
Oesterreich 1309-1559*). His intention to go to Zürich is mentioned in the report
of the spy and he had enough time for a visit there between October 16 and
November 8.

not expect acquittal and remission of penalty if he is shown to have broken the law. Again the veiled acknowledgement that a case could be constructed against him. Otherwise this letter repeats again in different form his sense of solidarity with his chosen community. This opposition to the authority of the feudal lords and the officials in Innsbruck is not his private feud as they might suppose. It is a movement of the people with whom he is bound up, and the fact that it is a movement of a number of communities gives its refusal the legitimacy for revolt which may not be accorded an individual. The specific point at issue, as in the first protest, is still the matter of restoring everything that Angerer claimed had been taken from him. But it has become the hook on which Gaismair now hangs the whole rationale for his resistance. Thus he writes:

> To begin with, since the demand of the Provost (Angerer) regarding the restitution of goods taken from him concerns the whole community of the towns and jurisdictions along the Eisack and all those related to them [in the revolt], who have covenanted with them, be it known that, because of the strength of their unity, they may in no way legally be separated. For this reason, according to our union with each other, I neither will nor may be separated from them since I am not their representative nor can I make promises for them. They have given me no right nor order as one man to speak for them all or in any way to enter into dealings concerning this matter...
>
> I therefore protest herewith that I am not obligated to appear before this court at this time in the absence of my comrades to reply to the charges against me since they have given me to right or direction so to reply and have themselves not been invited on appear.[240]

Obviously Gaismair is here not stating the theological justification for revolt, but he is clearly stating that the revolt is that of a whole community and that he will not be separated from it. It is "our"

---

[240] Anfänklich die weil des Probsts vordrung Antrift erstattung seiner genomen hab des Ain ganntze gemain Stet vnd gericht am Eysakh vnd alle Ire mitverwandtn so sich zu Inen verpunden habn zu hebn vnd zelegen beruert demnach In craft Ir verpindung Kain sonndrung aus rechtmessigem grund beschehen mag. Aus disem grund so kan noch Mag Ich der Ich Kain versprecher noch Vertretter der Andern bin Auch desshalben von Inen Kainen gwalt oder beuelch hab Ainig fur sy All Antwurt geben oder mich desshalbn ir handlung einlassen Souil mich Ainige Person neben allen meinen mit gewandten die Clag Antrift will ich mich nicht Jnhalt unnserer verpindung von Inen abgesonndert haben.
....
Darauf will ich hie mit protestirt habn das Ich nit schuldig bin diser Zeit vor disem Rechten mich Ainig in abwesen meiner mit gewondtn der gwalt oder beuelch Ich nit hab vnd sy fur Recht nit geladen sind Antwurt ein zelassen....

revolt, not "mine". Clearly it has given him safe and adequate ground on which to stand in his intentions.

One will not go far wrong in assuming that the letter was prompted by conversations he must have had with Zwingli before he wrote. Zwingli had helped him think through his problem and gave his actions a firmer theological base, for Zwingli had written several years earlier in Article 42 of his interpretation of the *Schlussreden* that if a hereditary king is a tyrant not just anyone should seek to depose him. That only produces rebellion which is contrary to Scripture. But if the people unanimously agree that he has to go, his deposition is legitimate.[241] The uncertainty which Gaismair had experienced earlier about his actions and which had been a factor in his repeated insistence on trusting Ferdinand and his Council was dispelled, for he now had, as it were, the approval of God for armed opposition to the sovereign. Gaismair's hope for help from Zwingli had therefore borne early fruit. This letter may therefore definitely mark his movement to the social and political theory of Zwingli. But even then he remained selective.

Benedikter's claim that in this letter Gaismair repeats his readiness to appear for judgement in Innsbruck under certain conditions is not supported by the letter itself.[242] Between October 9/10, the date of the earlier letter, and October 25 he had undoubtedly learned what was happening in the country, and how noble and prelate were exacting vengeance upon their defenceless subjects, frequently in complete disregard of the law. This letter, rather than being a renewed offer to appear in Innsbruck for judgement is evidence that Gaismair had quite given up the hope for justice from those in power. Thus before he ever got word that his request for safe-conduct had been granted he had determined not to accept it and this letter explains why. His action is therefore not mysterious nor even morally questionable, for there is no doubt that had he accepted the offered safe-conduct, it would have meant his early death. The letter demonstrates again Gaismair's legal expertise and his continuing concern for legal procedure in achieving justice. It is written evidence of how a man was gradually pushed into uncompromising revolt by deliberate, calculated perversion of justice on the part of Ferdinand and his Council.

---

[241] *ZSW* II, 345.

[242] Benedikter evidently simply took over Hollaender's assertion. Hollaender refers to the letter in *Der Schlern* 13, 380, but has the sequence of events so confused as to be entirely unreliable.

Hermann Holzmann's statement that in those days the government also sinned must surely be the most remarkable understatement in all the writing about Gaismair.[243] The fact that this protest was not delivered in Innsbruck until November 14,[244] strengthens the argument advanced earlier that Gaismair was in Zürich when he wrote it, and adds weight to the claim that he did not intend to appear in Innsbruck now.

That Gaismair's conclusions were fully justified is shown also by the Diet which met on October 30 in Bozen to elect the Tyrolian delegates to the Austrian Diet which was to meet in Augsburg. There was not one single reference to the Diet of Innsbruck where it had been decided that the sovereign would hold worldly power of the church in trust until a council could be called. Yet at Bozen the clergy again took their place as the first estate with barely a ripple of protest. Macek writes very much to the point: "Even while the poor subjects were tortured because they refused to recognize the validity of the Innsbruck *Landtag*, the estates gathered in Bozen flagrantly disregarded the decisions made there without any penalty." [245]

Perhaps the months of reflection on what had happened to him, to his family, and to his country, and his ceaseless planning for further action had built up in him the pressure of revenge which becomes evident in a conversation Gaismair had with a spy who masqueraded as a supporter early in January, 1526. Gaismair was then at Klosters near Davos.[246] Unwittingly he revealed to the spy all the chief components of the plan he and Zwingli had drawn up for the attack on Tyrol in April.[247] What is of importance now, however, is not the detail of the planned invasion but the burning spirit of vengeance which is expressed in his words. The nobles, the towns, and any in the communities who have lent money to the sovereign to pay for the mercenaries who now oppress the land will get their own back.[248]

---

[243] H. Holzmann, *op. cit.*, 464.

[244] This is indicated above the address on the outside of the letter.

[245] *Macek I*, 347-349.

[246] TLRA *HR 106*, 232-233.

[247] See page 57 above.

[248] In August, 1525, the government decided to raise money for the suppression of the revolt by making a *Landesanleihe* paying 5% interest. The nobility and all who had means were expected to contribute to the loan. (*Macek I*, 328). A typical request, tantamount to an order, went to the bishop of Brixen for a loan in the amount of five thousand Rhenish guilders in cash or silver plate whichever was most convenient. He is warned not to make any excuses (AVB, *Urkunde 17694*, dated Sept. 4, 1525).

Their names are all marked on a sheet of paper, for he knows exactly what is going on in the land. His surging sense of the injustice done him which had dispossessed him and his family, made exiles out of them, and hurt his friends and relatives is transmuted here into the resolve to avenge the injustice indiscriminately upon everyone who had even a minute part in it. This desire for revenge was to be his constant companion for some time.

5. Gaismair's Exile and the End of Violent Revolt

On November 13 Ferdinand wrote to the Council in Innsbruck giving his formal approval for the proposed safe-conduct for Gaismair.[249] Ten days later he sent a letter to the mayor and Council of Zürich, requesting the arrest and imprisonment of Gaismair, if he should be there, according to the extradition agreement.[250] Ferdinand's spies had reported that Gaismair was planning to go to Zürich.[251] The safe-conduct for Gaismair was finally made public on December 8 and sent to the magistrate at Sterzing who was to pass it on to Mrs. Gaismair so that she could get it into his hands.[252] But Ferdinand was not satisfied. Even while the safe-conduct was in effect he suggested that some of the officials along the border with the Grisons should meet and plot to get Gaismair dead or alive, but at this point the Council appeared to have an attack of good conscience and suggested that it would prejudice their honour to do this.[253] Now Ferdinand was sorry that he had agreed to the safe-conduct ruse. It was too slow for him. He instructed the Council on December 15 to find out secretly whether Gaismair had received the safe-conduct. If not, they were to recall it so that he could be proceeded against by assassin.[254] Also on December 15 he wrote again to Zürich that if they apprehended him with the safe-conduct he should immediately be

---

[249] TLRA *TE*, 426.

[250] Schadelbauer, *Tiroler Heimat* N. F. III, 1930, 90-91.

[251] Letter of November 7, 1525 of the Count of Montfort to the Council in Innsbruck, TLRA *HR 106*, 92.

[252] TLRA *TE*, 443v-444.

[253] TLRA *VKM* I, 269v-270; *AFD* II, 75v-76.

[254] TLRA *VKM* I, 276. On Dec. 19 the Council wrote to the magistrate at Sterzing to find out whether the safe conduct had been delivered, and whether Gaismair had accepted it (TLRA *TE*, 458), and on Dec. 22 the Council reported to Ferdinand that they had not been able to find out. Again they pleaded not to pursue him while under safe conduct since it would prejudice Ferdinand's honour (TLRA *AFD* II, 87).

released; if without it, to hold him until he could be brought back by his officials.[255]

From Zürich Gaismair had gone back to the Grisons to a place named Fideris early in November.[256] The area in which the town lay formally belonged under Habsburg authority, but the Habsburgs were especially hated there and the people had successfully refused to pay the feudal dues as well to do formal homage to Ferdinand. There was widespread commitment to Reformation teaching.[257] Gaismair was there among friends. In December he apparently went to Zürich again and stayed there until early in 1526 when, feeling his life threatened by Ferdinand's henchmen, he returned to the Grisons and settled down in Klosters, where his family soon joined him. [258]

Gaismair's time with Zwingli had been used to forge plans for the liberation of Tyrol from Habsburg tyranny. The relatively unknown "Plan zu einem Feldzug" prepared by Zwingli at the end of 1525 [259] and the report of a spy transmitted to the Council in Innsbruck by Jacob Trapp, royal administrator (*Pfleger*) at Glurns, on January 24, 1526 [260] together reveal the configuration of a military alliance of international dimensions which had a real chance of success. This called for a coalition between the cities, Zürich, Berne, St. Gall, Constance, and Lindau [261] with the Grisons. They, together with an army Gaismair would collect and all under Gaismair's command, would attack Tyrol when France and Venice started the war against the Emperor during his absence in Spain before Easter. The union of evangelical cities was to be Zwingli's work. Gaismair had in fact received assurances of support from France and Venice.[262] The point of attack was to be the little city of Glurns just inside Tyrol.[263] After that, Gaismair knew, the population of the Etsch and Eisack valleys would rally to him and the conquest of Tyrol would be virtually

---

[255] Staatsarchiv Zürich, *Beziehungen zum Ausland: Österreich, 1309-1559.* Unpaginated.

[256] See note 251.

[257] Benedikter, *op. cit.*, 132-133.

[258] Letter of Andreas Walch, magistrate in Sterzing, to Council Jan. 2, 1526, TLRA *HR* 106, 235; 233.

[259] *Huldreich Zwinglis Sämtliche Werke* Bd. III, ed. E. Egli *et al*, Leipzig, 1914, 539-583. Hereafter referred to as *ZSW*.

[260] TLRA *HR* 106, 232-233.

[261] This is also supported by the confession of Hans Gaismair early in April, in a letter of the Council to Ferdinand April 7. TLRA *AFD* II, 241-243.

[262] TLRA *HR* 106, 232-2.

[263] Letter of Council to Jacob Trapp, April 8, 1526, TLRA *TE*, 559v.

certain.[264] He had gradually collected about him a well-equipped, disciplined army of about 700 men from the Grisons, the Allgäu and Tyrol.[265]

Sometime early in 1526 Gaismair prepared his justly famous Constitution (*Landesordnung*).[266] It represented the program for which his army was to fight. More detailed reference to it will follow below. For now it is sufficient to say that it is a remarkable document for its time, anticipating as it does a completely new and different social order. Other peasant programs assumed the continuation of the feudal order and called simply for removal of abuses. Gaismair calls for a complete break with the past. Günther Franz writes: "Taken as a whole the *Ordnung* is the work of an idealist, who, as he himself says 'in all things he did not seek his own advantage, but firstly the honour of God and then the common good.'" [267] While it bears clear marks of reformation influence it goes far beyond Luther and Zwingli, for both of them would have rejected it with horror had it been offered to them as a true expression of evangelical faith. The title of one extant copy of the *Landesordnung* reads: *Michael Gaysmairs unchristliche greuliche Ordnung vnnd vnvillich Erschrockhenlich auch on mennschlich furnemen gegen der F. Gr. Tirol.*[268] That is characteristic of the true revulsion of the powerful and privileged against Gaismair's program. Gaismair's plan for the conquest was serious business. Hans Gaismair later confessed that they wanted to conquer "the whole land," to "kill all the nobles, clergy, burgers, and all who belonged to the honourable estates," and to "rule the land according to their own desire." [269]

The agitation in Tyrol continued, the radical clerics playing an important role in keeping revolutionary ideas alive. In the major centres of the lower Inn Valley as well as in Sterzing, Brixen, and

---

[264] Letter of the magistrate of Sterzing to the Council Jan. 23, 1526, TLRA *HR* 106 (unnumbered). Also *AFD* II, 247.

[265] Letter of Wolf D. von Ems to Council May 2, 1526, TLRA *HR* 106, 228.

[266] Printed by Hollaender, *Der Schlern* 13, 1932, 425-429, and reprinted in Kaczerowsky, *Flugschriften des Bauernkrieges*, Hamburg: Rowohlt, 1970, 79-83. See English translation in Appendix I, pp. 131-136.

[267] Franz, *Der Deutsche Bauernkrieg*, 1933, 263. Writer's translation.

[268] AVB, Urkunde no. 16575 "Michael Gaismair's unchristian, horrible order and unjustified, terrifying, and inhuman intention against the royal domain of Tirol." See also Ch. III, note 6 below.

[269] Letter of the Council to Veit Wähinger Apr. 11, 1526, TLRA *TE*, 566v.

Meran they openly continued their agitation.[270] All openly challenged church doctrine. Some went so far as to call for complete destruction of all ecclesiastical and secular authority.[271] There are repeated indications of the widespread sale of heretical books especially at the Bozen fairs, and of the eating of meat during Lent.[272] In addition there are numerous reports of general unrest among the people also in the Inn Valley.[273] The government was very reluctant to prosecute vigorously and had to explain repeatedly to an impatient and angry Ferdinand that the situation was too tense for strong measures. Ferdinand for his part could not see any reason why the mercenaries now stationed everywhere should not be used to force compliance.[274]

Gaismair had become Ferdinand's permanent nightmare. He could not wait for the safe-conduct term to expire, but kept pushing the Council to get Gaismair dead or alive. Plans for assassinating him were made in January, 1526, the first in a long series of at least one hundred such attempts, and a price of three to four hundred guilders was promised for bringing in Gaismair alive and two hundred guilders for bringing him in dead.[275] Plans for diplomatic action to achieve the surrender of Gaismair, detailed plans for kidnapping and murder followed in dizzy succession, only to fail utterly.[276] Involved were nobles and churchmen, as well as criminals who were promised complete pardon if they would bring him down. Gaismair for his part was well aware of these attempts and went about accompanied at all times by a bodyguard of twelve men.[277]

Gaismair had laid his plans for the attack of Tyrol well, but shortly before the date set Zwingli withdrew his support because he was under pressure from the Catholic cantons. Moreover the whole plot became known when Hans Gaismair, having talked too much, was

---

[270] The references to these peace disturbers are too numerous to list here. Representative loci are: *TE* 437v, 463v-464, 497: *AFD* II 82-84, 86, 239f, 240v. Correspondence between Ferdinand and the Council on this matter passed every few days. Dates of the references are Nov. 8, 1525-Mar. 31, 1526.

[271] TLRA *VKM* I, 278f; *HR* 106, 68; *TE* 597.

[272] TLRA *VKM* I, 314; *TE*, 518.

[273] TLRA *CD* I, 265f, 266v-267.

[274] TLRA *VKM* I, 322v and *AFD* II, 82-84, 240v.

[275] Council to Jacob Trapp, Jan. 30, 1526, TLRA *TE* 494v-495. See also *VKM* I, 294v-295.

[276] TLRA *TE*, 498, 503-503v, 542v, 543f; *AFD* II, 104, 124-5, 239, 240-241; *VKM* I, 301v-302, 307v-308.

[277] TLRA *AFD* II, 260f.

arrested, and a complete confession extracted from him under torture.[278] This narrow escape drove the authorities to frenzied activity
to bring Gaismair in, again without success.[279] But Hans Gaismair,
his brother, was executed in Innsbruck on May 28.[280]

Gaismair immediately began planning further. Firm contact with
refugees from the Allgäu who were in Appenzell strengthened his
force.[281] His attention now focused on a renewed outbreak of the
revolt in the Pinzgau in Salzburg territory. Accordingly, writes
Macek, Gaismair set out with his army from Appenzell on May 2.[282]
Their way lay through the Grisons, and then, in small groups through
the Etsch and Jaufen valleys to Sterzing where Gaismair solicited
and got considerable support.[283] From there they moved with a peasant guide [284] over the Pfitscherjoch into the Ziller Valley and then
over the Gerlospass into the Pinzgau,[285] where the small groups arrived about the middle of May.

This trek was a remarkable performance at a time when the snow
still lay deep on the high passes and mountain trails, and when spies
and mercenaries were everywhere. But it was accomplished with such
secrecy that the officials were about a week late with attempts to
intercept them. The first intimation that they knew of Gaismair's
coming is dated May 22, and the day after a decree was published
promising one thousand guilders for producing Gaismair alive and
five hundred for producing him dead.[286] On May 25 the Council shared
the bitter news with Ferdinand, excusing themselves by explaining
that "The mountains and the roads in this land are such that people
who come unannounced can easily come in and pass through [un-
noticed]." [287] Ferdinand's reply is dated June 1. He called for all who

---

[278] TLRA *TE*, 556, 559v-560, 562-563; *AFD* II, 241-243, 248v-249.
[279] Especially an attempt to negotiate his surrender with the *aman* of Klosters,
TLRA *AFD* II, 253f; and Ferdinand's frustration at its failure *VKM* I, 335v-336.
[280] TLRA *AFD* II, 277.
[281] TLRA *HR* 106, 228; letter of Council to city of Bludenz TLRA *Buch
Walgau* I, 196v, 50; *TE*, 609f; *AFD* II, 262f. All these references dated May 2-8.
[282] *Macek I*, 405.
[283] Benedikter, *op. cit.*, 153.
[284] TLRA *CD* II, 66-7.
[285] TLRA *TE*, 633.
[286] *Ibid.*, 631v-633. This was a fabulous sum of money at a time when a labourer
earned 1.60 guilders and a carpenter 2.50 guilders a month (Benedikter *op cit.*
221). See also *Buch Walgau* I, 50v.
[287] TLRA *AFD* II, 274v. "... wan es sind dermassen gebirg und weg in
disem Land daz dergleichen personen so ungewarnet sachen jrem zug nemen
leichtlich durch passiren vnd hinein komen mogen."

aided Gaismair on the trek to be punished and raised the price for him to one thousand guilders dead or alive.[288]

Gaismair had in the meantime taken over command of the peasant siege of Radstadt. But temporary successes could not prevent the collapse of the revolt due primarily to the strength of the forces of the Swabian League who came to the Archbishop's aid. On July 1 the peasant force under Peter Pässler was defeated and scattered.[289] News of the defeat evidently prompted Gaismair to give up the siege of Radstadt, for on July 2 a certain Hofstetter reports to Caspar Kunigl that Gaismair and Pässler had joined forces.[290]

They now had to decide what to do because they could not face the overpowering forces of the Swabian League. It appears as though Gaismair had made some advance preparations for just such an event as this. On June 23 the Council in Innsbruck wrote to Eglof Schell announcing that a letter from a contact in Lienz stated that Gaismair was planning to go to Lienz and from there to invade the country by way of the Puster Valley.[291] On June 26 Caspar Kunigl was warned that Gaismair was coming.[292] Gaismair's reason for looking in that direction was the forming of the League of Cognac including France, Pope Clement VII, Venice, Milan, and Florence, and directed against Charles V. This league had been formed at the instigation of Francis I of France as soon as he was released from his imprisonment in Madrid following his defeat at Pavia. It put Charles in a critically vulnerable position. All in whom the Emperor had formerly placed his confidence, his pope from the house of Medici, his royal "brother" Francis I, his Duchy of Milan, and even England, a silent partner, were now against him. The imperial army in Italy remained unpaid and un-

---

[288] TLRA *VKM* I, 358.

[289] BTFD *Codex 1182*. Letter of Burckhart von Ems, commander in the Pinzgau from Puessendorf on July 1. *Codex 1182* contains a collection of documents and letters mostly addressed to or concerning vice-regent Leonhard von Völs between the years 1520-1526. Some of these deal with the Peasants' Revolt. The title page of section II of the codex indicates that these materials come from the archives of the castle of Prösels, the seat of Leonhard von Völs. Macek was evidently unaware of this material, for he used secondary sources extensively in this section. The materials have no page or folio numbers but are bound in approximately chronological order.

[290] *Ibid.*

[291] TLRA *TE*, 682v.

[292] *Ibid.*, 687v. The letter referred to by Schell is probably the one mentioned in TLRA *CD* IV, 53 where a young woman is identified as the carrier.

cared for.[293] Tyrol, the heartland of the Habsburg empire, was especially vulnerable to invasion at this point because of its common border with Venice. All this Gaismair knew. It is no wonder that he felt justified in finally acting upon his invasion plans at this point. The defeat of the peasant cause in Salzburg must have added to his determination finally to achieve something. News of military movements by Venice on the southern border of Tyrol gave Gaismair the confidence that open hostilities against the Habsburgs would soon begin and that his dream of meeting the hated foe on equal terms would soon be fulfilled.[294] He had made advance arrangements with Lienz at this time to be allowed into the city without opposition.[295]

Accordingly on July 6, an army of about two thousand men crossed the Taurer Alps at a height of nearly eight thousand feet over difficult and little-known mountain paths that led directly to Lienz.[296] The army entered the city unopposed, having strict orders not to molest anyone or to take anything. The city provided them with food and drink without charge.[297] There, at a public meeting of the whole force it was decided to take over the Puster Valley and from there the whole of Tyrol. The army then moved in forced marches to Silian to besiege the fortress of Heunfels and get hold of the arms and munitions stored there.[298] Kunigl tried to raise a force against Gaismair but was unsuccessful since the people sympathized with the invaders.[299] He was unable to face Gaismair with the meagre forces he had and simply sat still in Bruneck.[300] Heunfels could not be taken and the march continued. On July 9 the force passed Innichen and moved up the valley in direction Sterzing.[301] In Kunigl's letter to Brandisser of July 9, he urges the strengthening of the fort at the Mühlbach defile. This cannot have been achieved since Gaismair must have arrived at

---

[293] Karl Brandi, *Reformation und Gegenreformation*, München: Bruckmann, 1969, 155, 178.
[294] *Macek I*, 424-5.
[295] This can be concluded from the letter to Schell on June 23. See note 292.
[296] Letter of Council to Leonhard von Völs, July 8, 1526, TLRA *TE*, 699f.
[297] Confession of Hans Schwaiger, TLRA *HR* 106, 45.
[298] TLRA *AFD* II, 305f. For the castle as a munitions depot see E. Widmoser, *Tirol A bis Z*, Tyrolia-Innsbruck, 1970, 278.
[299] TLRA *AFD* II, 305v; AVB *Urkunde 14696*.
[300] BTFD *Codex 1182*: letter of Caspar Kunigl to Anton Brandisser July 9, 1526. Sparber's claim that Gaismair could not take Bruneck because there were 1100 mercenaries there may well be accurate. It would simply mean that Gaismair and Kunigl were both convinced that they could not defeat the other and therefore avoided engagement.
[301] *Ibid.*, TLRA *AFD* II, 396v-397.

the defile before the letter got to Brandisser at Rodeneck. Hans Schwaiger, one of Gaismair's men, later confessed that they had been tempted to storm the fortification because it was only lightly defended,[302] but they apparently decided not to risk the army nor to take the time required for its capture. They therefore bypassed it to the right over the mountain toward Meransen.[303] From here they intended to move on Sterzing but their way was blocked by a force from Innsbruck, Hall and Sterzing under the command of the feared Jörg von Frundsberg.[304] Thus Gaismair turned south and went to Lüsen, a friendly village near Brixen, where another public meeting of the whole force was held to determine further action. While the pugnacious farmers of Rodeneck were anxious for the army to attack Brixen,[305] the people of the Puster Valley, albeit friendly, had shown no heart for further fighting. Gaismair's expectations of a general rallying behind him had not materialized. The people had evidently resolved to continue their protest against feudal oppression by passive rather than violent resistance.[306] Gaismair now put the question to his followers as to whether they should face Frundsberg and the further prospect of the Swabian League forces, or continue the fight from Venetian asylum.[307] In any event they swore an oath to God and all the saints that they would stay together and commit all they had to plunder and kill all the clergy and the nobility. The decision was to go to Venice.[308]

On July 9 Ferdinand wrote from Speyer that Gaismair must be caught and a price of one thousand to sixteen hundred guilders was offered.[309] It was in vain. On July 12 the army crossed intact into the

---

[302] TLRA *HR* 106, 47. AVB *Urkunde 27334* in the volume *Generalraitung 1525-1527* records payment to mining magistrate Lorentz Gruber at Klausen for 59 men he sent to the fortress to protect it against Gaismair. It is dated July 10, 1526.

[303] TLRA *AFD* II, 306v.

[304] *Ibid.*; *Franz Schweyger's Chronik der Stadt Hall v. 1303-1572*, 1867, 87. Benedikter devotes considerable space in his book to delineating the life and personality of this able commander.

[305] Confession of Michael Gall, TLRA *HR 106*, 190-191.

[306] The Pustertal had not joined in the violent uprising of May 1585 in spite of vigorous efforts of Gaismair to enlist their support. Gaismair's expectations therefore appear to have been unrealistic and determined more by the wish than by reality. It may not be without significance that the area between Bruneck and Brixen had the greatest concentration of Anabaptist activity several years later, a movement dedicated to nonviolence.

[307] The expected hostilities of the League of Cognac had not begun as Gaismair had expected. Here too he may have been led by the wish, at least so far as the timetable was concerned.

[308] Confession of Christoph Kopf, TLRA *HR* 106, 47.

[309] TLRA *VKM* I, 384.

Republic of Venice after a swift march through Tyrol.[310] Again official intelligence lagged far behind events for it was not until July 13 that the Council reported to Ferdinand that Gaismair was on his way to Venice.[311] Only on July 22 was Innsbruck certain that Gaismair was out of their reach on Venetian territory.[312] On July 18 Gaismair rode to Venice with a delegation of thirteen farmers to offer his services to the Venetians and ask for protection and aid; the offer was accepted and the request granted.[313] He was taken into Venetian service as a captain of mercenaries and sent into hostilities before Milan.[314] Gaismair also immediately made it his business to get mercenaries from Switzerland for Venetian service.[315]

By thus making common cause with the opponents of Habsburg ambition Gaismair ensured failure for his plans. His tragedy was that he could not realize his aims by himself with the small army he had, but by attaching himself to those with more power he was depending on a phantom. For none of the allies of the League of Cognac were even remotely interested in Gaismair's vision of a new social order. Aiding him in its realization would have meant the creation of a source of social infection dangerous to the order they stood for. But they were ready to use him as a welcome pawn in their own plans.[316]

---

[310] *Macek I*, 431. All the dates cited are supported by the sources. That provides the following amazing result. The route that Gaismair travelled from Innichen to Agordo on the Tyrol-Venetian border is no less than one hundred miles through high mountain terrain. On July 9 he was in Innichen and three days later on July 12 in Agordo. That means a daily march of thirty-three miles plus the stop in Lüsen and including at least two mountain passes of six thousand feet each. To take an army of two thousand on such a march without losses in such a short time speaks eloquently for Gaismair's military ability and his gift for leadership. The words of the chronicler Kirchmair referring to this event therefore become quite credible:

> Jedoch sag ich, daz Gaismair der erst gewesen ist, der mit gewalt so weitt durch das Lannd gezogen ist. Man wolt wol sagen, er hiett mit den gerichten etwas ain Verstannd gehebt, angesehen daz er vor in der Emporung Ir haubtman gewesen was. Vnnd diser des gaissmairs Zug machet ain Wunder grossen schrecken im Lannd, Warlich gleich als wär es doch ain besonndere plag von got uber das Lannd verhenngt. (*Op. cit.*, 477).

[311] TLRA *VKM* I, 387f.
[312] TLRA *AFD* II, 315v.
[313] TLRA *CD* I, 289.
[314] *Macek I*, 442.
[315] *Ibid.*, 443.
[316] This is clearly revealed by the fact that the French sent reports of Gaismair's activities to Innsbruck, TLRA *CD* III, 10-11. Even Zwingli who was certainly not a cynic in the French or Venetian style, was governed ultimately by his own interests and held to Gaismair only if it was compatible with his own designs. This was shown in the spring of 1526 and again in 1530.

The Venetians found him useful as a means of tying up Habsburg forces inside of Tyrol which might otherwise have stood against them in Italy, and were glad to accept the help of his well-disciplined and at times substantial army.[317] Demonstrably they had no interest in invading Tyrol or even in aiding Gaismair to do so.[318] The other allies likely regarded him as little more than a welcome *condottiere* in Venetian service. The excellence of his service and his ability is extensively documented [319] but it was ultimately wasted effort. The paradox of Gaismair as an ally of the Pope was evident to Innsbruck. The Council wrote to Ferdinand on July 23 that the Pope ought to be informed about the anticlerical and antiecclesiastical stance of Gaismair as clearly revealed in his Constitution.[320]

All of this so perceptive a man as Gaismair must have sensed, and the truth of it must have been his constant unwelcome companion. He must have known that in spite of his international reputation he was but a small fish in the muddy pond of international diplomatic intrigue. But he could not give up. He continued, naively, to hope that his faithfulness in Venetian service would finally merit their support for the realization of his vision.[321] He lacked the cynicism requisite for success in international affairs which is to his credit. But he continued to work for his remaining years at the hopeless task like Sisyphus, for to give up meant despair. His undimmed vision must have been for him the justification for the otherwise hateful occupation of constantly procuring mercenaries, especially from Switzerland, for the Venetian Signoria. For until they could be marshalled to liberate Tyrol they were fighting for the preservation of an order which his soul abhorred.

His hope was especially strong during the first year in Venetian service. He recruited mercenaries in Germany, Tyrol, and Salzburg,[322] and he had great hopes that if he attacked, the subjects of Tyrol would flock to his aid.[323] Early in 1527 he wrote to contacts in Bozen that he

---

[317] *Macek I*, 440, 443, 444, 448, 452.

[318] *Ibid.*, 448-449, 454-455. The French also cautioned Venice against supporting any revolutionary activity on the part of Gaismair, *Ibid.*, 449. See also TLRA *HR 106*, 112-113, 190-191.

[319] See note 317.

[320] TLRA *AFD* II, 317v-318.

[321] *Macek I*, 447, 450.

[322] TLRA *CD* I, 341f., AVB, *Codex XI, Bischof Georgen von Österreich Registratur Gemainer Sachen de annis 1527-1530.* 23-24.

[323] TLRA *HR 106*, 190-191, 168-170.

was planning on eating the Passover lamb with them that Easter.[324] Although Gaismair discontinued his military services to Venice in August, 1527,[325] he continued to recruit mercenaries for the Signoria. Thus he was in the Prättigau and the Grisons in May and June 1528 with the intention of bringing back ten thousand men.[326] Knowledge of his presence there prompted Innsbruck to redouble efforts to assassinate him.[327] Particular hopes fastened at this time on Sebastian Nusch, a former rebel, who was promised full pardon plus the total reward of at least one thousand guilders for the murder of Gaismair.[328] On August 14 Ferdinand, writing from Prague, set the new price for Gaismair dead or alive at one thousand guilders plus a pension of four hundred guilders per annum for life.[329] Alarms about a possible attack of Gaismair on Tyrol with Venetian help sounded constantly and kept Tyrolian authorities in constant fear of invasion and a new uprising.[330] His contacts with Zürich continued.[331]

Late in 1529 Zürich attempted to win the support of Venice for a renewed anti-Habsburg league. The League of Cognac had just been dissolved by the Peace of Barcelona between Emperor and Pope. For Zwingli this meant the possibility of a combined front of the two against the evangelicals.[332] Thus Phillip of Hesse, Ulrich of Württemberg, Venice, France, and Zürich were seen as a possible new coalition to oppose the Emperor. Gaismair introduced the Zürich emissary to the Signoria in Venice to initiate negotiations. His old hope for international aid was renewed, since the projected hostilities provided for an invasion of Tyrol with a decisive role for himself.[333] Innsbruck became aware of the new development almost immediately including

---

[324] AVB Rathsprotokoll 1515-1527, 774.

[325] Macek I, 455.

[326] TLRA Buch Tirol II, 50, 51v-52, 54v-55, 60; Buch Walgau I, 204, 67f; HR 106, 158.

[327] TLRA Buch Tirol II, 50, 51v-52, 54v-55.

[328] TLRA HR 106, letter of Oct. 7, 1528; AKM III, 248v; Buch Tirol II, 62; VKM II, 247.

[329] TLRA VKM II, 247.

[330] TLRA CD II, 12 (Mar. 1527); HR 106, 112-113. (Sept. 1527); VKM II, 89f. (Sept. 1527); Buch Tirol II, 67v (July, 1528); CD II, 260 (August 1528); Buch Tirol II, 75 (Aug. 1528).

[331] TLRA Buch Tirol II, 60, 73v-74 (June-Aug. 1528), and 110, 114 (May-July 1529).

[332] Letter of Council to Ferdinand, Jan. 6, 1520, TLRA AKM IV, 2v; Macek I, 473-475.

[333] O Vasella, "Ulrich Zwingli und Michael Gaismair, der Tiroler Bauernführer," Zeitschrift für schweizerische Geschichte, 24, 1944, 409, note 61.

the specific purposes of the new coalition, namely that it was directed against the Emperor's religious policy.[334] However, this renewed anti-Habsburg plan also dissolved before it could become effective, for neither Venice nor France would commit themselves to it.[335] But Innsbruck was kept in suspense by the renewed efforts of Zwingli and Gaismair to keep an anti-Habsburg front alive by themselves during the summer of 1530.[336] On August 19 the Council wrote to Leonhard von Völs that the plan was to field three armies. Zürich would field one, Lindau, Constance and some other imperial cities another, and Gaismair a third one of eighteen thousand comprised of Italians and Germans.[337]

That letter also carries the news that Zürich had conferred citizenship on Gaismair. However, a letter of the Council to Marx Sittich von Ems on October 8 states specifically that the diplomatic efforts of von Ems in Zürich had prevented the conferral of citizenship on Gaismair, and that in view of the existing situation that was no mean achievement.[338] Since this is a later communication it can be assumed that the earlier assumption based on the letter to von Völs was erroneous, and that the plan to give Gaismair citizenship was not carried out.[339]

But these latest plans for an attack on Tyrol also collapsed because of disunity among Protestants and the pressure of the Catholic cantons on Zwingli.[340] Gaismair stayed in Zürich until the end of the year 1530 which accounts for the continued communications concerning a possible joint attack of the Swiss with Gaismair. On January 1, 1531 the Council even instructed Marx Sittich von Ems about what to do if Zwingli showed up in Innsbruck jurisdiction.[341] Only on March 15 a letter to von Ems indicates that the threat had subsided.[342]

---

[334] TLRA *AKM* IV, 2v, letter of Council to Ferdinand, Jan. 6, 1530. This is a correction on Macek's statement on page 478 that Innsbruck heard nothing about these plans until after the coalition had collapsed.

[335] *Macek I*, 478.

[336] TLRA *Buch Tirol* II, 170f. (July 9); *Buch Walgau* I, 209v-210 (July 20).

[337] TLRA *Buch Tirol* II, 189, 194; *Buch Walgau* I, 88.

[338] TLRA *Buch Walgau* I, 90. Neither O. Vasella nor J. Macek seems to have been aware of this communication.

[339] This judgement was confirmed by a search in the Staats- and Stadtarchiv in Zürich. The register of conferred citizenships in the Stadtarchiv makes no mention of Gaismair. The author was assured that it was therefore legitimate to assume without question that Gaismair had not become a citizen there.

[340] *Macek I*, 481.

[341] TLRA *Buch Walgau* II, 91. Letters of Jan. 4, 21, Feb. 17, 91v-92v, 94-94v indicate the continuing belief of Innsbruck in a possible attack from the west.

[342] *Ibid.*, 94v.

Some comments must be made at this point on a few isolated sayings attributed to Gaismair and spoken after the failure of the revolt and the abortive invasion of 1526.

He is reported to have said to some Allgäu farmers in the spring of 1526 that it was not his intention to harm anyone, nor to rob anyone, but only to protect the Gospel and give it his aid.[343] This is the first of the two times that Gaismair is reported to have used the term "Gospel". Again, it sounds like a Zwinglian formulation, for Zwingli had taught that it was one of the duties of a government to make room for and promote the Gospel. But the statement adds nothing to what has been said above.

Only two other statements of Gaismair are known, one from 1527 and one from 1528. We will discuss them together at this point in the interests of a simpler organization of the material. This procedure will slightly change the chronological sequence, but this will not affect its proper understanding. The first is reported by Heinrich Mardeburg on February 19, 1527. While in the hospital at Meran he heard of a letter which Gaismair had written to friends at Bozen in which he had promised that "he would eat the paschal lamb with them." [344] This statement bears strong resemblance to a word of Jesus in Luke 22:15: "How I have longed to eat this Passover with you." (Zwingli: "Mich hat herzlich verlangt, dies Osterlamm mit euch zu essen . . ."). If he is indeed adapting a word of Jesus here, it is the only time he brings him into the picture. Perhaps it testifies to a rising interest in the New Testament and especially the person of Jesus. But the word could also be an echo of Joshua 5:10, the account of the first passover celebration of Israel in Canaan. In either case it is one more testimony that Gaismair did think and speak in biblical terms.

The second statement comes in the report of a spy which was forwarded to Innsbruck on May 18, 1528. Gaismair and a preacher from Zürich were travelling from Venice to Baden in the Argau where they were to negotiate about getting mercenaries of which the Venetians stood in need. When they stopped at an inn in the Prättigau they were recognized by their clothes as coming from Italy, and some local farmers asked if they knew anything about Gaismair. After a

---

[343] Confession of Adelhaid Gaisser made end of May 1526, Franz L. Baumann, *Akten zur Geschichte des Deutschen Bauernkrieges aus Ober-Schwaben*, Freiburg, 1877, 405. ". . . sy sin mainung nit, niemant zu beschedigen, noch nichtz zu nemen, sonder allain das ewangeli zu beschiermen vnd dem selben ain bistand zu thuen."

[344] AVB *Rathsprotokoll 1515-1527*, 774. "Der Gaissmair hab heraus geschribn denen von Bozen Er well das osterlamp mit Inen essen. . . ."

moment of uneasiness Gaismair revealed his identity to the farmers and said: "... I do not deny my identity where people know about me or ask about me, for I am neither a thief nor a murderer but an honest, upright godfearing man and have no need to deny my name. For because of the Gospel I must avoid my Fatherland." [345] This is the only passage in which Gaismair specifically refers to himself as godfearing to counteract the official claims that he is a thief and a murderer. More than two years after the Constitution he still identifies his actions and aims as being identical with the Gospel. The term Gospel is for Gaismair synonymous with his vision of social justice for Tyrol including his plans for its realization. It has therefore little resemblance to Luther's or even Zwingli's use of the term. It is also likely a synonym for Word of God which he used in the Constitution. He is in exile because of his intention to found a new Christian order in Tyrol. He has therefore not yet given up hope of realizing his vision.

Since late 1527 Gaismair had lived on an estate in the suburbs of Padua. The Signoria had granted him an annual pension of three hundred ducats in appreciation for his services so that he could live comfortably with his family.[346] In August 1530 it was suggested in Venice that his pension ought to be withdrawn because he was a heretic. However he also had defenders so that it was not done.[347]

On April 15, 1532 Gaismair was roused out of bed early by an acquaintance under the pretext of a business deal. The fabulous bribe offered by Ferdinand had made traitor of a friend, and when the unarmed Gaismair appeared in answer to the summons, he was killed by dagger thrusts.[348] But the Council in Innsbruck had become so accustomed to doubledealing that the murderers probably never got the fabulous reward promised so often. Ferdinand, however, was determined to keep faith this time, for as late as August 1533 he was

---

[345] Letter of Steffan Baly to Balthasar von Ramschwang, May 18, 1528, TLRA *HR 106*, 162-162v. "... ja ich lougnen sin nit wo man mich kennt oder mir nach fraget Dan ich bin weder ain dieb noch ain morder vnd bin ain fromer redlicher erlicher man vnd darff mich mins namens nutz zeverlougnen Dan ich mus von des Ewangelis wegen min vater land miden."

[346] *Macek I*, 463.

[347] E. Wieser and H. S. Schubring, *Studien zu den Film Michel Gaismair*, Archival-arbeit Italien-Innsbruck, 1943, 5. German translation of Marino Sanuto, *I Diarii*, LIII, col. 400.

[348] *Ibid.*, 20-23.

still angrily ordering the Council to pay the reward.[349] For his part
he had become so accustomed to his nightmare that even after Gaismair's confirmed death he wrote to the Council to do whatever they
could to find out about Gaismair's plans.[350]

[349] TLRA *AKM* V, 184; *VKM* IV, 161v-162, 185v-186, 223f, 251v-252v.
[350] TLRA *VKM* IV, 39f. (Apr. 29, 1532).

CHAPTER TWO

MICHAEL GAISMAIR'S RELIGIOUS AND SOCIAL VIEWS

When, in approaching the task of presenting Gaismair's religious and social views, we compare the materials available for a study of the thought of Gaismair with those relating to his contemporary revolutionist Thomas Müntzer, we find ourselves at a distinct disadvantage. A whole volume of materials from Müntzer's own hand is available today in critical edition. Gaismair's only ideological writing, his Constitution, amounts to no more than five printed pages. The task of presenting a detailed and comprehensive portrayal of Gaismair's thought is therefore beset with difficulties, since we are driven to depend much more on inference from what we know about Gaismair's life from the events in which he was a major participant; and from the general socio-religious situation of the day.

In addition to his Constitution we have the three letters from the hand of Gaismair written on June 19, October 9/10, and October 25, 1525, comprising about six printed pages. Further there are about twenty-five lines of spoken statements attributed to Gaismair by his followers and from the reports of spies. There is thus a sum total of no more than twelve printed pages of firsthand materials available to date, and there is little likelihood of anything else turning up.

As to secondary materials they fall roughly into three groups. First there is the information relating to Gaismair's family home, the events of his life and his activities, all found in the archival holdings referred to extensively above, a few of which have appeared in print. Secondly there are the materials relating to the religious and social situation of the day, including information about Gaismair's employers vice-regent Leonhard von Völs and Prince-bishop Sebastian Sprentz of Brixen, and the grievance submissions of the Tyrolian people. The third group can be broadly defined as Reformation influences. This includes Reformation writings, association with radical preachers, and Gaismair's contact with Huldreich Zwingli and the Tyrolian Anabaptists.

1. SUMMARY OF GAISMAIR'S RELIGIOUS AND SOCIAL VIEWS PRIOR TO THE CONSTITUTION

We have discussed Gaismair's social and religious views especially in the analysis of his letters above. Before proceeding to analyze the Constitution it is necessary to make a summary of his views up to this point.

All the basic ingredients of his thought are already present and will only be strengthened and confirmed by what follows.

The very first intimations we have about Gaismair's views, the famous marginal notes, reveal his towering sense of justice and his determination to see justice prevail in Tyrol. This was to be a main mark of the man until his death. He was outraged at the inequalities of the existing judicial system for it discriminated against the poor and weak. He held the view common among contemporary social dissidents everywhere that all men are equal and should therefore have equal right to justice.

Basic to this sense of justice was Gaismair's fervent belief in God, specifically the God of the Old Testament. This belief guided his thinking and action to the end. He had an unshakable conviction in the inevitability of retribution for wrong done and of reward for righteousness. Faithfulness to God consisted for him in faithfulness to his neighbor in the exercising of social justice. It had little or nothing to do with abstract theological ideas such as justification by faith which were so important to the Reformers. Godlessness was for him not some separation from God because of wrong belief or sacramental exclusion. Rather he saw it simply as social unrighteousness and the perversion of justice. For Gaismair even a sacramentally ordained priest was godless if he oppressed the poor.

Gaismair's religious and social views flowed into each other. He could conceive of no system such as Luther's doctrine of the two kingdoms which separated the two.

Of great importance in his thought was Gaismair's view of his own role. He had a sense of being chosen as God's instrument for avenging the oppressions and the wrongs he saw around him. The revolt, he wrote to bishop Sprentz, was not man's but God's work, that he himself was caught up in it, and that he could not resist it. He saw himself involved in it by divine design. Just prior to his planned invasion of Tyrol in March, 1526, he regarded himself as a new Moses, leading the dispossessed into their own land and making a completely new beginning. His sense of justice and his vision of his own role in establishing justice came from the Old Testament and he appropriated Old Testament models to embody it as we shall see.

Nevertheless, he was initially a very conservative revolutionary.

He regularly appealed to the existing constitution and law and to the decision of the Diet. He trusted Ferdinand and cooperated with his officials. He warned his people against fomenting another revolt since it would involve a lot of bloodshed. He wanted a new social order by negotiation and constitutional change. It was only the continued subversion of justice by the royal council and Ferdinand against Tyrol and himself that made Gaismair an advocate of the total abolition of the existing social system.

He seems to have struggled with the very idea of revolt. Drawn into it after it began, and taking over the leadership, he immediately applied the brakes and brought order to the movement. His continued confidence in Ferdinand and the constitutional process made him a reluctant revolutionary. But all that changed when he saw only continued injustice. Under the influence of Zwingli he developed a rationale for revolt which included tyrannicide. Zwingli had written that only a total community may seek to overthrow an existing government. Gaismair's second letter to the royal council reveals this line of thought when he stoutly defends his solidarity with the peasant communities and that his case can in no way be separated from theirs. By this time he was radicalized to the point where he was prepared to exterminate all who opposed his vision, including the archduke, thus giving expression to the view that the only way to save the revolution was by making a total break with the past.

Like almost all social revolutionaries from the Middle Ages onwards he became violently anticlerical. He saw the clerics as the mainspring of the perversion of justice and vowed that they would all have to be killed before things improved. It is therefore to be expected that he rejected the old church in toto and called for its total exclusion from secular power. His vision for the new Tyrol included the church, but in a clearly defined and limited role.

We can therefore see that already before the writing of the Constitution his thinking and action was shaped by the Old Testament. The New Testament has practically no place in his system of thought, a fact which will be confirmed by a close study of the Constitution.

2. THE NEW RADICAL PROGRAM

Along with his activities of gradually building a revolutionary army and nurturing widespread support for his planned invasion, Gaismair had to give careful thought to the formulation of a program. He knew he could not go into a renewal of the rebellion with the uncertainties of the summer before. He knew that his convictions about priorities and his vision of the goal that was to be fought for would have to be written down so that it could be shared. Sometime in February or March he wrote down his so-called Constitution (*Landesordnung*).[1]

This Constitution is a document unique for its time. It is of a completely different order than the other peasant programs of the time, all of which dealt with the removal of abuses, but left the basic feudal order untouched. This last was true of the Meran Articles as well, even though they aspired to a new constitution. Gaismair's Constitution provided for a totally new social order. After all the influences which played on Gaismair before and during this time have been considered it becomes clear that he had no model from which he worked. It was a totally new departure. For this reason alone Gaismair's part in the Peasants' Revolt deserves greater attention than it has received until now. As Macek writes, it represents a revolutionary program which called for the total abolition of the domination of the ecclesiastical and secular feudal lords and the placing of all power into the hands of the people.[2] Günther Franz refers to it as the most utopian attempt to erect a Christian social order,[3] and Benedikter calls it one of the most significant state utopias ever conceived.[4]

a) *The Constitution and other peasant programs*

Gaismair's Constitution must first be looked at in the context of other peasant statements that had been drawn up between November 1524 and May 1525. It is highly likely that he was acquainted with at least some of them, especially those from the Allgäu. All of these statements were earlier than Gaismair's. The question of possible dependence upon them is therefore a legitimate one.

Some elements were common to the whole movement. An obvious

---

[1] *Macek I*, 370. The text of the Constitution was published in a critical edition by Hollaender in *Der Schlern* 13, 1932, 427-429. It was reprinted by Günther Franz, *Quellen zur Geschichte des Bauernkrieges*, 1963, 285-290, and also by Klaus Kaczerowsky in *Flugschriften des Bauernkrieges* in the Rowohlt series *Texte deutscher Literatur 1500-1800*, 79-83. There is a previous English translation by Jacob Schapiro *Social Reform and the Reformation*, New York, AMS Press, 1960, pp. 147-151. It is, however, inaccurate at a number of points. See Appendix I.

[2] *Macek II*, 190.

[3] Franz, *Der Deutsche Bauernkrieg*, 1972, 158.

[4] *Ibid.*, 253. "... dessen Landesordnung zu den hervorragendensten Staatsutopien vieler Jahrhunderte zählt..."

case is the concern for the faithful preaching of the clear and pure Word of God without any human admixture.[5] Another is the disposition of the tithe which is to be used for the support of the pastor, the poor, and any community emergency, in that order.[6] Several times we encounter the aim that all is to be done for the glory of God and the love of the neighbor.[7]

The *Allgäuer Bundesordnung* and the *Allgäuer Artikel* which, with the exception of the Meran Articles, were geographically closest to Gaismair, reveal only three parallels with the Constitution. These are the emphasis on obedience to authority, the faithful preaching of God's Word, and the mutual pledge to commit life and property to the peasant cause.[8] At the point, therefore, where one might expect more parallels there are only a few, no major ones among them.

One other statement deserves mention here which shows interesting parallels to the Constitution. It is Friedrich Weigand's Draft for the Reform of the Empire (*Reichsreformentwurf*). It appeared in May, 1525, in Franconia, geographically removed from Gaismair. Franz asserts that nothing came of the proposal because of the advance of the Swabian League.[9] It is doubtful that Gaismair saw it.

The document is interesting in that it too is a kind of constitution drawn up as a possible program for the reform of secular and religious matters. The relevant parallels are intriguing. Weigand, like Gaismair later, calls for common and uniform measures and weights, a new currency, and the outlawing of the great commercial and banking companies like the Fuggers.[10] There are to be no more beggars in the land, and the buildings of the clerics and orders are to be converted to uses for the common good.[11] The first three and the last are the most important but all of them would have occurred to so fertile a mind as Gaismair's as he thought about the economics of his new order. In any case, there is not a shred of evidence that Gaismair knew Weigand or that he depended on him in the writings of his Constitution. Moreover, Franz claims that Weigand's proposals had only a minimal relation to the peasant movement, nor did Weigand

---

[5] Franz, *Quellen*, 169, 194, 197, 198, 201, 291.
[6] *Ibid.*, 176, 265-6, 300-301.
[7] *Ibid.*, 240, 329.
[8] *Ibid.*, 196, 197, 166.
[9] Franz, *Der Deutsche Bauernkrieg*, 201.
[12] Franz, *Quellen*, 374.
[11] *Ibid.*, 372.

look for a totally new order as Gaismair did.[12] Finally, if it could be shown that Gaismair borrowed from Weigand it would still be only a few relatively unimportant points.

A special word needs to be said about the relation of the Constitution and the Meran Articles. Macek denies that Gaismair had anything to do with them and bases himself on the difference between the profound radicalism of the Constitution as over against the relative conservatism of the Meran Articles. The fact is however, that the Meran Articles were produced in May 1525, nearly a year earlier. At that time they accurately reflected Gaismair's own point of view before he himself became radicalized as has been described above. The resemblance between the Constitution and the Articles is so striking at a number of points that one must allow for the real possibility that Gaismair had a hand in the formulation of the articles. Any apparent dependence on the articles has been acknowledged at the proper place.

Thus while there are similarities between Gaismair's Constitution and other peasant statements, there appears to be no critical dependence by Gaismair on any of these.

Virtually all the writers who comment on the Constitution acknowledge Reformation influences on it to a greater or lesser degree. There can be no question, especially about the influence of Huldreich Zwingli, the Swiss reformer, upon it especially in terms of specific measures embodying social justice. This will be dealt with in detail in the course of analyzing the Constitution.

b) *The biblical orientation of the Constitution*

First of all we must raise the question of its overall orientation. A close examination reveals that Gaismair's Constitution is basically biblical in orientation although it entirely lacks the numerous biblical references so customary in writings of the time.[13] Sometime early in

---

[12] Franz, *Der Deutsche Bauernkrieg*, 200-201. Another comparison might be with Johann Eberlin von Günzburg's "Wolfaria," numbers 10 and 11 of his *Fünfzehn Bundsgenossen.* (*Die Sturmtruppen der Reformation: Flugschriften der Jahre 1520-1525*, Darmstadt: Wissenschaftliche Buchgesellschaft, 1974, 51-54, 125-160). While both Günzburg and Gaismair present visions of a new order, there are very few specific similarities. Günzburg is basically a proponent of conservative reform like Weigand; Gaismair is a radical revolutionary. See also Ferdinand Seibt, *Utopica*, Düsseldorf: L. Schwann, 1972, 70-81.
[13] An evident reason for the omission of biblical references may well be that in documents of this kind they were not customary. The Meran Articles did not have them nor did similar documents such as the *Allgäuer Bundesordnung* (March

1526, perhaps during the time that Gaismair was working on his Constitution he said to a group of farmers from the Allgäu that "he would lead them into a good, plentiful land, in which no one would be against them, but all would stand together with them." [14] Macek was aware of the poetic nature of these words and interpreted them to be a reference to an imaginary land which could be anywhere where oppression had been removed and the Gospel was freely heard.[15] But that does not fit in well with Gaismair's practical turn of mind, nor is it likely that he would have held before his exiled peasant revolutionaries so indefinite a goal. Gaismair was speaking about Tyrol and he was speaking about it in biblical terms. The poetic nature of the words can be accounted for by regarding them as free quotations from the books of Exodus and Deuteronomy. Exodus 3:8 reads: ". . . to bring them up out of that country into a fine broad land; it is a land flowing with milk and honey." [16] While this passage makes no reference to plenty it is certainly implied. Other passages specifically refer to the land as being rich.[17] In Deuteronomy 8:7-9 we have a description of Canaan that is at the same time a remarkably accurate description of Tyrol.

> For the Lord your God is bringing you to a rich land, a land of streams, of springs and underground waters gushing out in hill and valley, a land of wheat and barley, of vines, of fig trees, and pomegranates, a land of olives, oil and honey. It is a land where you will never live in poverty nor want for anything, a land whose stones are iron ore from whose hills you will dig copper. You will have plenty to eat and will bless the Lord your God for the rich land he has given you.

In Deuteronomy 7:24 and Joshua 1:5 we are told that "no man will be able to withstand you." These words are the likely basis for Gaismair's statement that "no one would be against them." [18] That Gais-

---

7, 1525) or the *Bundesordnung der Bauern in Oberschwaben* (March 6, 1525). In fact the Twelve Articles represent an exception among peasant statements with their marginal references.

[14] From the confession of Agatha Käss, May 1526, F. L. Baumann, *op. cit.*, 407. "Sagt mer, der edelman hab in allen sovil vertröst, da er sie in ain gut, vol land furen wöll, do niemant wider sie, sonder jeder meniglich mit in vff sein werd," There is no compelling reason for placing this statement in April as *Macek I*, 404 does, since there is no clear chronological point of reference in the confession.

[15] *Macek I*, 405.

[16] The Luther translation reads: ". . . und sie ausführe aus diesem Lande in ein gutes, und weites Land, in ein Land, darin Milch und Honig fliesst."

[17] Deut. 1:25; 4:21.

[18] Luther: "Es wird dir niemand widerstehen."

mair was talking about Tyrol to those farmers in biblical terms may be regarded as certain, especially since, as we shall see immediately, the Constitution itself clearly reveals wide dependence on the Bible and particularly upon the book of Deuteronomy.

In the third article of the Constitution Gaismair states that they will agree to "erect a wholly Christian order, founded in all things solely on the holy Word of God, and to live by it completely." [19] On the basis of these words one could justifiably assume that the Constitution itself would be based "solely on the holy Word of God." In fact that turns out to be the case and if Gaismair did not add the references he well might have since in most specifics precise biblical documentation can be given.

The covenant upon which the exiles are entering on the basis of this Constitution is not to further individual interests but firstly to promote the glory of God and then the common good. This formula is present in the preamble to the Meran Atricles as well as the *Allgäu Bundesordnung* of March 7, 1525, the only two documents that can seriously be considered as having influenced Gaismair at this point. Since however Gaismair himself participated in preparing the Meran Articles it is safe to assume that they are the model he worked from. In addition, since Gaismair was working with a Deuteronomic model he would have found this formula implied in the twofold division of the Decalogue which provides for the sole glory of God in the first part and the laws for the common life of the community which benefit everyone else in the second. The words of the Decalogue appear in Deuteronomy 5:6-21.

This basic commitment to God's glory and the common good will insure God's grace and aid (Deuteronomy 5:32-33). God is to be trusted for he is completely true and trustworthy and deceives no one (Deuteronomy 32:4) (art. 1).

Article 2 speaks about the complete extermination of those who persecute the "eternal Word of God." Isaiah 40:8 is the bestknown Old Testament passage proclaiming the eternality of God's word, a passage understandably very popular for the Reformation. But if we consider Gaismair's thinking here in terms of Deuteronomy the whole article can be understood as a restatement of God's command to exterminate the inhabitants of Canaan (Deuteronomy 7:1-2), allowing of course for adaptation to the specific circumstances Gaismair had

---

[19] "ain ganntz cristenliche satzung, die allein in allen dingen aus dem heylligen wort gottes gegründt ist, auffrichten und daran genntzlichen geleben wellet."

in mind. There is some justification for taking the term "the godless" to mean the priests, since Gaismair used the term in that sense in his protest of October 9/10. In that case the specific basis for this article may be 2 Kings 23:5 where Josiah is reported as having suppressed the heathen priests who made sacrifices at the hill-shrines.[20] The New Testament provides many passages referring to persecution for the sake of the Word of God (Matt. 13:21; Matt. 5:11-12; I Peter 4:12-16).

The third article is a commitment to live and act only according to the Word of God since they have come into the possession of Tyrol, a clear restatement of the words of Deuteronomy 6:23-25. "But he led us out from there to bring us into the land . . . . The Lord commanded us to observe all these statutes and to fear the Lord our God . . . . It will be counted to our credit if we keep all these commandments . . . as he has bidden us."

Special privileges of wealth and power will be abolished, he writes in article 4, since they lead to the perversion of justice. The great passages from Isaiah (5:8-23, 10:1-4) and Amos (5:7-12, 6:2-6, 8:1-7) in which these prophets denounce the oppressions of the rich and powerful by which the poor lose their rights and possessions quickly come to mind.

There is no biblical passage which orders the destruction of city walls and fortresses which Gaismair demands in article 5. But it is to be done in order to remove the inequalities which men have created. The article is therefore a call for the realization of the equality of all men. While there is no special passage in Deuteronomy which states that men are equal it is presupposed everywhere in the Pentateuch and certainly by the prophetic oracles referred to above. A number of New Testament passages refer to the breaking down of old divisions (Rom. 10:12; I Cor. 12:13; Gal. 3:28; Col. 3:11).[21]

Article 6 which calls for the removal of all images and shrines and

---

[20] It is also possible that the account of Josiah's reformation in 2 Kings 22-23 influenced Gaismair. In any event, biblical scholarship has demonstrated the integral relationship of that account with the book of Deuteronomy. Another possible source of authority is 1 Kings 18, the account of the extermination of the priests of the persecuting Jezebel by Elijah.

[21] Would it be too fanciful to suggest that perhaps the passage from Ephesians 2:14-15 in which Christ is said as having "broken down the enmity which stood like a dividing wall between them . . . so as to create . . . a single new humanity" was in Gaismair's mind in this article? Considering that Gaismair interpreted the Bible in a nonspiritualized concrete way this possibility is at least worth considering.

of the Mass because they are an abomination before God, are partially verbal quotations from Deuteronomy 7:5 and 25:

> ...pull down their altars, break their sacred pillars, hack down their sacred poles and destroy their idols by fire..... for these things are abominable to the Lord your God.

The faithful and truthful preaching of the Word of God is the concern of article 7. Here, too, Gaismair is echoing a concern frequently expressed by peasant statements. All sophistry and appeal to canon law is to be avoided.[22] Among the many passages in the New Testament dealing with the faithful preaching of the pure Gospel I Cor. 1:17, Gal. 1:11-12 are the most pertinent. The books of canon law are to be burned. This is perhaps based on the actions of Josiah, King of Judah, who in his reformation burned all the objects of idolatry (2 Kings 23). He may also have had in mind the burning of books of magic in Acts 19:19.

Articles 8, 9, 10, and 12 deal with the judiciary. Judges and jury are to be elected. Justice is to be dispensed locally, quickly, and justly. The biblical basis is unquestionably Deuteronomy 16:18-20:

> You shall appoint for yourselves judges and officers, tribe by tribe, in every settlement which the Lord your God is giving you, and they shall dispense true justice to the people. You shall not pervert the course of justice or show favour, nor shall you accept a bribe; for bribary makes the wise man blind and the just man give the crooked answer. Justice, and justice alone, you shall pursue, so that you may live and occupy the land which the Lord your God is giving you.

The appeal procedure of article 12 may be based on Deuteronomy 17:8-11, which provides for appeal to the centre of the nation. In article 11 Gaismair has located the centre of Tyrolian government in Brixen. It is there that the appeals will be heard. This is a clear reflection of Meran Articles 11 and 12 (Franz's enumeration).

The provison of a school in the capital for the teaching of the Word of God and only of that Word (Deuteronomy 4:12) in article 13 must be seen as a means to ensuring greater faithfulness in carrying out the mandates of Scripture. For from Scripture only "the justice of God may be clearly set forth."

Sections 14, 15, and 16 [23] deal with taxes, customs duties, and tithes.

---

[22] It is assumed that in this context "juristerey" refers to canon law.

[23] Gaismair's enumeration of the articles goes only to 13, why is not known. I have therefore identified the remainder by paragraphs, commencing at 14.

In section 14 dealing with taxes Gaismair mentions the "free year" referred to in the "law of God." This is likely a reference to Deuteronomy 15:1 which in the Luther translation speaks of an "Erlassjahr," a year of remission. The tithe, which was a sore point for peasants everywhere, was justified by Gaismair in section 16 as a law of God. This is commanded in Leviticus 27:30, but the references Gaismair has in mind are undoubtedly Deuteronomy 26:13-15 and 14:29, for these passages contain not only the command to give the tithe but also the use to which it is to be put, namely to support the Levites, the aliens, the widows and orphans. Gaismair follows the same order when he says that everyone is obligated to pay the tithe according to God's command and that it is to be used to support the preachers,[24] and whatever is left over is to go to the support of the poor and needy. Section 17 expands on the use of the tithe. That section also refers to the giving of alms which are called for if the tithe is not sufficient. A number of passages in the Gospels assume that giving alms is God-pleasing (Matt. 6:3-4; Acts 10:4), but in Luke 12:33 there is a direct command to do so (Meran Article # 10).

Sections 18, and part of 19 deal with administrative, agricultural and economic issues characteristic of Tyrol and no specific Scriptural texts can be adduced as basic to the provisions. They all proceed broadly from the basic principle of the common good.

The prohibition of the merchant's activities is motivated by the determination to observe the scriptural law against usury in Leviticus 25:36. Again it cannot be ruled out that Gaismair also thought here about Jesus driving the buyers and sellers out of the temple because of their dishonest dealings (John 2:16; Matt. 21:12-13). Part of section 10 and sections 20 and 21 then proceed to the new ordering of the commercial sector (Meran Article # 22).

Section 22 can be documented from Deuteronomy at several points. The concern for good relations with neighboring countries is an echo of Deuteronomy 4:6 since both passages use the key word *Verstand*. The provision for uniform weights and measures is directly based on Deuteronomy 25:13-16 (Meran Article # 18).

The 23rd section contains a reference to the great commercial houses of the time which have gained their wealth by unjust usury

---

[24] At this point Gaismair has the only references to the New Testament, specifically his legitimation for having preachers. The references are Titus 1:5 and 1 Tim 5:17.

and the shedding of human blood.[25] This is a clear reflection of Proverbs 1:10-16 where the shedding of blood is joined to robbery of the innocent. The prophets also connect the rapacious practices of the rich with shedding blood as for example Micah when he speaks of building Zion in bloodshed (3:10), and Jeremiah who writes: "But you have no eyes, no thought for anything but gain, set only on the innocent blood you can shed, on cruel acts of tyranny" (22:17). Those who enlarge their fortunes at the expense of the poor are under the judgement of God (Isa. 5:8-9). Sections 24 and 25 then deal with the proper ordering of the mining enterprise and its proceeds which have been reclaimed from the Fuggers and the Baumgartners, to the common good of the land and its people (Meran Article # 22).

We have thus been able to set at least 41 specific biblical references into the margin of Gaismair's Constitution, and more could be added if we followed the sixteenth century practice of including duplicates. In addition many general passages could be cited as well. We can therefore visualize Gaismair working at his Constitution with a well-used Bible open before him. His use of it testifies to a good knowledge, especially of the Old Testament which contains the Hebrew model of the unified religious-social-political community which he portrays in the Constitution. Macek's judgement that Gaismair was concerned to free himself from the Bible, unlike Müntzer, and thereby become more rationalistic and down to earth is therefore shown to be inaccurate.[26] It is true that he does little direct quoting, but to use that as the basis for concluding that he does not think in biblical terms has been shown to be unwarranted. Gaismair used the Bible precisely because it is down to earth and concrete. The main reason for omitting specific references would appear to be that the common man, for whom the Constitution was prepared, was not concerned with theological niceties. A plain, unadorned, direct presentation was what was needed. Besides, in the new Tyrol there would be no high clerics, humanistic merchants, or nobles sympathetic to the Reformation to convince with subtle arguments.

But we can say even more. Earlier it was argued that Gaismair had a sense of calling and destiny about himself. He was to be God's

---

[25] At this point (429, line 14) Hollaender has made a punctuation error, placing a comma after "erlangt", which makes the following clause difficult to decipher. Placing the comma after "gelt" allows intelligible reading of what precedes and follows.

[26] *Macek I*, 378.

instrument to bring God's justice to realization. That can now be more specifically described. "I will lead you into a good, plentiful land, in which no one will stand against you" he said to the Allgäu farmers. Tyrol is described in terms of Canaan and the laws which are to regulate life in the Promised Land are those chosen for Gaismair's Tyrol. From all this we may conclude that Gaismair cast himself in the role of Moses, called by God to lead a homeless group of fugitives from various countries into the rich land of Tyrol. He gives them the law, his Constitution which they agree to accept and live by. With God's help they will now militarily attack and conquer the "good and plentiful land," driving out and exterminating the powerful spiritual and secular oppressors. The people who hitherto had been oppressed and despised would now live safely, with no one to oppose them and dispute their rights. The new nation would order its life according to the justice and equity of God's laws. The claim that the Constitution is based consciously on a biblical model is made therefore not only on the basis of being able to supply biblical references for every part, although that is done as well, but depends primarily on the way Gaismair sees the Constitution, himself, Tyrol, and his plans for the conquest of Tyrol as a unity based on the model of Israel invading and subduing the Promised Land under Moses.

c) *Analysis of the Constitution*

As might be expected, the Constitution is the most productive of Gaismair's limited writings for knowledge of his views. There can be no doubt that *Landesordnung* was Gaismair's own work and that he meant this document to be the constitution for Tyrol. When he wrote it the long awaited Constitution which was to emerge from the Diet of 1525 had not yet been prepared.

While, as Günther Franz says, the Constitution was an accomplishment which had no literary antecedent, it is entirely obvious that Gaismair was not simply producing a constitution unilaterally. A number of the provisions of the Meran Articles went into the Constitution. By extensively using these articles, Gaismair was including specific concerns of the peasants which had been denied them at Innsbruck. In that sense therefore the Constitution was a community document. It thus spoke to the Tyrolian people with special force. Those who joined Gaismair committed themselves to its realization with everything they had. Having looked at the biblical orientation of the Constitution, we must now examine its provisions in detail and see what they tell us about Gaismair's own convictions. At the very outset the Constitution provides for a government to which faithfulness and obedience is pledged. Gaismair writes that this government is "set over them" (*fürgesetzt*). This reflects the Reformation interpretation of Romans 13 where Paul writes of the state as instituted by God. Zwingli had described the state as being, not an order of nature, but as directly instituted by God because of human sin, emphasizing that it is always subject to God.[27] But God has appointed it for man's good and that conviction becomes the mandate for obedience. Obedience to the state is one of the pillars of the new order. It is seen again, therefore, that Gaismair always thought in terms of an organized societal order, and not in individualist anarchist terms. The government is to be elected by the people, representing the whole land as well as the special social grouping of the miners (art. 11). There is no trace now of a sovereign; the political form will be republican like Zürich, but on a more broadly representative basis. There is little doubt that Gaismair adopted this model under the influence of his experiences in Zürich several months earlier; he had already determined to oppose Ferdinand, and the alternative form of government suited his determination to have the people participate directly in its function. Everything is to be done by common consultation. How much individual liberty would have been granted in Gaismair's land is a moot question. Ferdinand had insisted that the preaching of the Gospel must always be in the service of the state and never against it.[28] There is evidence to indicate that Gaismair thought so too. His bringing of evangelical clerics to Tyrol was done not only for the spiritual nurture of the people but to support his program of revolt and the new order. When in the fall of 1526 one of the Gaismair clerics apparently began to encourage some of Gaismair's men to leave Venetian service and go home, Gaismair summarily had him hanged on the nearest tree.[29] It is doubtful, for example, whether Gaismair would have been any more patient with the Anabaptists than Zwingli was.

The mutual commitment called for in article 1 is not for the satisfaction of any kind of personal ambition or advantage. This is an expression of Gaismair's passionate rejection of grasping for privilege for oneself at the expense of others, and contains far-reaching impli-

---

[27] *ZSW* II, 487; IV, 354-356.
[28] TLRA *TE*, 379.
[29] Wieser, *op. cit.*, 11.

cations for property and power and their uses. In place of the commitment to egoistic indulgence of power and property Gaismair calls for a new departure in the use of property and the power that goes with it. This people with its government would set the honour of God as its chief priority. God, the God of the Bible, is regarded by Gaismair as being over all. Everything in the Constitution depends first of all on the recognition that he is supreme.

While it hardly needs to be argued that this represents a Reformation position, it should be said that the Reformers rarely speak about God without at the same time speaking about Jesus. Unlike the Reformers, Gaismair never, in all his writings either directly or indirectly refers to Jesus. Nor does he anywhere with a single word refer to any personal religious experience such as those which Luther and Zwingli experienced. But this was precisely where the significance of Jesus came in. He had, according to the Reformers, fulfilled the righteousness which God demands and men can by faith participate in that righteousness. Thus Jesus was central for man's salvation from eternal condemnation. For both Luther and Zwingli the prescriptions of the Sermon on the Mount were mandatory for the individual believer. But both insisted that Jesus' prescriptions did not apply to the role of the magistrate and the conduct of the government. Now Gaismair's writings concern themselves almost exclusively with this aspect of human experience. When therefore he makes no reference to Jesus in this context he is simply doing what the Reformers did. The basic concern of government according to Zwingli, is human righteousness,[30] and for that the Old Testament provides the model. Israel's destiny was to glorify God by doing his will. It is clear that Gaismair had accurately understood this when he began his Constitution with the mutual pledge of government and people to seek the honour and glory of God before all else.

But it can justifiably be argued that the honour of God was primary also in official Catholic theory and that the Reformation had no monopoly on it. Where then lay the differences? They are both formal and material. Formally the Reformation removed the vast hierarchical mediatorial structure from between God and man by proclaiming the priesthood of all believers. The common man was thus moved as it were closer to God. The sole glory of God was no longer associated largely with the mediatorial church as bearer of the truth in its tradi-

---

[30] See A. Farner, *Die Lehre von Kirche und Staat bei Zwingli*, Tübingen, 1930, 39.

tion and liturgy, but much more immediately with the individual Christian and his direct relationship to God. Materially, at least for Gaismair, the glory of God is now to be expressed through the direct participation of the common people in the societal order which they were about to set up, the intermediary structures of the church and the state being held to a minimum. Not the church and the state in their sacramental essence now expressed the glory of God, but every man in his day to day life in the affairs and concerns of the new community.

That the glorification of God is expressed in the seeking of the common good is obvious, since the remainder of the Constitution concerns itself with a particular way of ordering and realizing the common good. The acceptance and commitment to carrying out this basic twofold demand of God as expressed in the Ten Commandments is the condition for the gracious aid of God. Men may safely rely on God's assurance of his gracious aid if they are obedient since he has repeatedly promised it, but more because God only is completely truthful and beyond all deceit. Gaismair is here simply expressing the Hebrew conviction that God's commitment to aid and bless his people is conditional upon their obedient fulfilment of his commandments.

This is perhaps the point at which the use of the terms reformed and Reformation, which have until now been used rather broadly, should be more carefully defined as they relate to Gaismair. Although Gaismair works in the Constitution with an Old Testament model, he does not see himself as restoring a Jewish community, but repeatedly identifies his vision as Christian. He states again and again that everything is to be done according to the Word of God. He makes provisions for the true preaching of the Word of God (he never uses the current term Gospel (*Evangelium*) in the Constitution). But nowhere does he speak of Jesus, as already indicated, and nowhere is there even so much as an allusion to the basic proclamation of the Reformers that man is sinful, that he has no merit of his own which can justify him before God, and that man is justified by faith alone as a gracious gift of God.

Gaismair should therefore once and for all be dissociated from Luther. Luther would certainly have disowned Gaismair on the same ground on which he refused to accept the program of the peasants in Germany, namely their claiming of the Gospel for their demands for social betterment. Luther's judgement on Gaismair, had he had the occasion to make one, would certainly have been that he was either a Jew or a Papist, but certainly not a Christian. When therefore Gaismair's ideas are still spoken of as reformed it is the Zwinglian expression of reformed thought and action that is meant. But Gaismair cannot be said to be a Zwinglian without extensive qualification either. The relationship of Gaismair and Zwingli will be spelled out as we proceed.

It is Gaismair's intention to establish a total Christian order based in all things on the holy Word of God (art. 3). He uses the terms holy Scripture, divine law, and Word of God interchangeably. The strong appeal to Scripture in the Constitution is certainly in part a consequence of his stay of several months in Zürich where his commitment to the Bible acquired earlier was strengthened and his knowledge enlarged.

In article 2 Gaismair refers to "the eternal Word of God" (*das ewig wort gottes*). Perhaps one should not read too much into the adjective eternal. But Gaismair expressed himself so succinctly and economically that its choice is perhaps deliberate. It could be a variant of the very common "the eternal Gospel" which is found in Revelation 14:6, and which was a very popular reference to the Gospel in the sixteenth century, especially in radical circles. It comes into use through writings attributed to Joachim of Fiore,[31] was used by Müntzer, and occurs in the writings of Hans Hut, the Anabaptist. It refers to the Gospel behind the written word, that which is quite beyond human manipulation. Perhaps Gaismair uses it here in the sense that it is not to be identified with any human interpretation, and therefore precisely for that reason opposed to the church's definition of the Word of God.

Fortunately we are not left only with general suppositions in seeking the roots for Gaismair's commitment to Scripture, for during the time that Gaismair was in Zürich, Zwingli's school for the training of ministers had just begun to function. Every day in the choir of the *Grossmünster* or in the chapter house systematic exegesis of the Old Testament took place involving Hebrew, Greek, Latin, and German, and the respective experts in those languages.[32] Auditors were admitted to these sessions and it is most likely that Gaismair partici-

---

[31] "Joachim von Floris," *Wetzer und Weltes Kirchenlexikon*, Freiburg, 1889, VI, Col. 1471-1480; A. S. Turberville, *Medieval Heresy and the Inquisition*, London, 1964, 35-37.

[32] O. Farner, *Huldreich Zwingli*, Zürich, 1954, III, 555-560.

pated in these "prophecies." The fact that only the Old Testament was studied at this time may in part account for Gaismair's almost exclusive use of the Old Testament. However, the book of Deuteronomy was not studied until early 1527,[33] so that Gaismair either came onto its importance for him by himself or else he was directed to it privately by Zwingli.[34]

Since the life of the whole new community was to be based exclusively on Scripture provision had to be made for some way of acquainting everyone with its provisions. Gaismair therefore included plans for a school to be located in Brixen (art. 13). It was to be staffed with university trained Bible scholars and it was to concern itself only with the study of the Bible. There seems little doubt that at this point too he was following Zwingli. For Zwingli had written in his *Auslegen und Gründe der Schlussreden* that "the divine Word is to rule over all men. It is to be set out before them, repeated and faithfully explained to them. For we are obligated to fulfil it." [35]

But Zwingli also provided a concrete model. Since 1523 Zwingli had been planning the founding of the school referred to above to train young men to be effective preachers of the word of God. On September 29, 1523, the Council issued a *Schulordnung* in which the purpose and something of the character of the proposed school were specified. Learned, able, and upright men were to read and teach the Scriptures every day, an hour each for the three biblical languages. There was to be no charge for this instruction since it would contribute to the honour of God and the common good through the capable service of the preachers trained there.[36] The school came into being in the summer of 1525, when Zwingli finally succeeded in securing the qualified teachers he wanted, in the form of the *Prophezei*, the daily study of Scripture already referred to above. Only the Scriptures, using the original texts plus the Vulgate were studied there.[37] The same provision is made for Gaismair's school. Only the Scriptures are to be studied. Zwingli's practice of studying only the Scriptures is rooted in his view that the Holy Spirit alone gives the

---

[33] *Ibid.*, 558.

[34] In his work on "Divine and Human Righteousness". *ZSW* II, 487, Zwingli specifically bases himself on the Old Testament when he discusses the establishment of human righteousness or justice, which is what Gaismair is principally concerned with.

[35] *ZSW* II, 521.

[36] O. Farner, *op. cit.*, III, 398-401.

[37] *Ibid.*, 551-553.

receptive reader the right understanding. This position is advanced against the claim of the Roman church that the Scriptures could only be understood with the help of the church, that is, the interpretations of the Fathers, the Councils, and the traditions. But the sole dependence upon these interpreters was, according to the Reformers, the cause of the false interpretation accepted by the church as correct.[38] Hence the concentration on the Scriptures only in the original languages.

Apart altogether from the theological basis of the argument, the rejection of the authorities of the Roman church would have been sufficient for Gaismair to follow Zwingli at this point. But Gaismair also specifically states that the divine justice, which is to be the law in the new Tyrol, can be discovered only in the Scriptures. The divine law is set over against the law of the exploitive and unjust feudal law which had been baptized into a divinely instituted order by the church. Gaismair's concern for the exclusive use of the Scriptures is therefore his concern for a totally new social order in which the authorities of the past are summarily rejected and the authority of the Word moved into their place. The Scriptures represent an authority that cannot be trifled with or changed at the whim or caprice of a powerful noble or prelate. And to avoid that danger from creeping in again, the old interpreters with their sophistic and juristic tricks are to be forever banned (see article 7).[39]

If Gaismair was using Zwingli's model here, a model that spoke to his own prior convictions, then Macek's judgement that the interpretive authority was no longer to be the church but the university is going beyond the evidence.[40] The implication is that this was a move towards secularism, the liberation from Christian tutelage. But in the sixteenth century the universities functioned very much as religious and not secular entities. Gaismair likely simply followed Zwingli here in the conviction that the Scriptures were clear in and

---

[38] ZSW II, "Auslegen und Gründe der Schlussreden," art. 1, 21-27.

[39] The rejection of sophistry is a common phenomenon in the Reformation era. All the Reformers were concerned with it as were the Anabaptists. But the uncertainty about the ways of the contemporary interpreters of Scripture is found also in Catholicism. The same chronicler, Kirchmair, who was so horrified at Gaismair and his activities writes, almost in anguish one feels, "Lass dein pitters leiden an uns durch verirrung deiner gelerten nit verlorn werden" (op. cit., 453). (Let not Thy bitter suffering be lost to us through the straying of Thy learned men.)

[40] Macek III, 131.

of themselves and needed merely the clarification of the languages. Ultimately God himself was the interpreter.[41]

Although Gaismair nowhere says so, it is likely that the purpose of the school was also taken over from Zwingli. It was to train men for the competent and true preaching of the Word of God. The preachers were key people in the movement headed by Zwingli, and Gaismair had himself learned that lesson some eight or ten months earlier when he had brought preachers into Brixen and Sterzing, some of whom at least were Zwinglians. But now a native breed of preachers was to be raised in the new school of Brixen. In Zürich the old Cathedral school had become a powerful force for change; Gaismair envisaged the same thing for the Cathedral school in Brixen. Until then it had served primarily as a conservative force, available primarily to the wealthy and powerful for the strengthening of their positions. Now it was to serve "the honour of God and the common good."

But the school was to have one other role, very important for the constitution and functioning of the new Tyrol. For three teachers from the school were to be members of the government along with the elected regents. Their function was to see to it that all decisions of the government were in fact in accordance with the commands of God as becomes a Christian people. Gaismair must have observed that the roles of Zwingli and Leo Jud in the affairs of state in Zürich were just that, and that a very determined attempt was made there to do everything according to the Scriptures. But he also learned of Zwingli's frustrations with the Council, and of his reluctant submission to the Council's caution when he would have liked to move more quickly in the work of reform.[42] Perhaps for this reason Gaismair included the three teachers as full members of the government. Thus he sought to provide the greater assurance that the commands of God would be known as well as carried out in the centre of power. One may even suspect that the number three corresponds to the experts in the three languages in the Zürich school. The three languages were seen as essential to the understanding of Scripture. Zwingli had written

---

[41] The short step was the move even among the Reformers to official interpretation, in their case of the educated leadership, when it became evident that a variety of interpretations of the supposedly clear scriptures began to emerge. This was a serious and thorny problem for the Reformers since it gravely imperilled their principle of the priesthood of all believers.

[42] Zwingli would like to have abolished the Mass before he did. It was not until 1528 that the Catholic members of the Council were finally expelled and he had a more unified Council to work with.

that only a true Christian could be a just magistrate, for only such a person could recognize and accept the ultimate base of government, namely the righteousness of God. Such a government alone would create and promote unity and stability among the people. "His kingdom is the best and most secure who rules alone with God." [43] The Christian magistracy therefore appealed to Gaismair's long-standing passion for social justice.

But before all that could be done the "godless people, who persecute the eternal World of God, oppress the common man, and counteract the common good" must be exterminated and put away (article 2). By "godless people" Gaismair almost certainly meant the clergy in the first instance.[44] The extermination of the clergy had been determined by a number of peasant leaders in Brixen in May 1525, and Gaismair had himself uttered such threats. His experiences with the prelate Angerer had made him more certain than ever that such men would cease to be dangerous only when they were dead. It was not only his personal hate and desire for vengeance which prompted this solution, but also his conviction that the clerics were the most incorrigible perverters of justice. No just order could emerge until they were utterly gone. But the rest of the feudal powerholders, including Ferdinand, were certainly also in his mind in this article.

He would also have gotten strong support from Zwingli at this point, for at the end of 1525 or early 1526 Zwingli wrote the first of his military operations plans the *Feldzugsplan*.[45] This work grew out of Zwingli's growing conviction that the Gospel would triumph under the prevailing conditions only if the evangelicals adopted the offensive, if need be militarily. In his work on "Divine and Human Righteousness" Zwingli had written that one function of the state (*Obrigkeit*) was to protect the church so that it could carry out its function of spreading the kingdom of God, and to see that the hindrances to the truthful proclamation of God's Word are removed.[46] That was written in 1523. By 1525 the threat to the church and the hindrances to the Word of God came not only from within but also very much from the outside in the form of the gradually developing Catholic resistance. For Zwingli it came most directly from the Catholic cantons,

---

[43] *ZSW* II, 473, 346. "Des rych ist aller best und vestest, der allein mit got herschet."

[44] See p. 49 above. See also Zwingli's strong words against monks and clerics in *ZSW* II, 298-304.

[45] *ZSW* III, 539-583.

[46] *ZSW* II, 507, 524. A. Farner, *op. cit.*, 49.

but also from the growing threat of imperial determination to carry out the Edict of Worms. Zwingli's concept of the role and obligation of the Zürich Council began to expand and the first *Feldzugsplan* is the draft of military action to remove the hindrances to the Gospel beyond the cantonal borders. Once it had been accepted that resistance to the Gospel should be eliminated by force, it was a short step to the call for total extermination of the people who resisted. Thus Gaismair could justify his murderous intentions against the prelates and feudal lords, not only in his innate sense of injustice which called for vengeance, but also theologically.

In Gaismair's vision of the new Tyrol the church and society are in no way separated, and nowhere is there any theoretical statement about the relationship of the two. One gets the impression that this question did not exercise him since in any event he was writing a constitution in advance. Perhaps he felt that that could be dealt with when the new state was set up, as is certainly the case with some other issues. That the church or at least the community of Christians was of basic importance to him is beyond question. He refers to the *cristenlich volckh* (Christian people) who will establish a *cristenliche satzung* (Christian order or law) and do away with all unchristian conditions. It should have become clear by now that Christian was synonymous in Gaismair's mind not with some abstract theological doctrine but with a just social order. What is just and right is Christian. The term is therefore used by him in a restricted and special sense. His notion of church should be seen and understood in this context. If Gaismair worked with the concept of church at all (he never uses the term to denote a new structure) it was the *Volkskirche* concept used in an undifferentiated way.

Again we can presuppose Zwinglian influence, but only in general terms. Zwingli was critical in his concept of church, but it was likely the actual situation in Zürich that influenced Gaismair. He must have known that the citizens of Zürich were compelled by order of the Council to have their children baptized,[47] and that the removal of images and the abolition of the Mass had come about by action of the Council. What Gaismair saw in Zürich was a functioning Christian order in which clear separation of any separate jurisdictions of church and state was not visible. The new Tyrol is a single unit, a Christian people in which neither "church" nor "state" are separate units. It

---

[47] This order was issued on Jan. 18, 1525 to deal with the dissidents later called Anabaptists.

will therefore not do to say, as Macek does, that the preachers were now only servants of the secular power,[48] since the power is not in fact secular but Christian. They were servants of the people.

Even though Gaismair was concerned with a new society and not merely church reform, a separate discussion of church reform and the role of the church is undertaken here in the interests of ordering the material. The first specific provision is the removal of all images, wayside crucifixes and all chapels that are not parish churches (article 6). This involves the abolition of the veneration of saints and all religious rites that are not related to the purpose of the parish church, which is the preaching and hearing of the Word of God. Similarly the Mass is to be abolished since it is an abomination before God and quite unchristian. It is to be done away with not simply because it is nonimportant but precisely because it is unchristian. It was therefore not a secondary matter for Gaismair. What was truly Christian was of basic importance to him.

It is at this point that Zwinglian influence has been most readily claimed. And indeed, when Gaismair was in Zürich the churches were austerely empty, devoid of colour and ornamentation. Even the organ had been removed from the *Grossmünster*. The churches served as places of assembly for hearing the Word of God and remembering the death of Christ in the bread and wine. For the Mass too had gone and in its place was a simple rite of commemoration with bread and wine. In place of the vessels of gold and silver Zwingli had insisted on using wooden cups and plates. Thus Gaismair saw with his own eyes a new, different, and simple kind of church life which undoubtedly appealed to him. Zwingli had rejected the claim that the images taught the people the Gospel. They do no such thing, he wrote; rather they create confusion. Men are to be taught by the Word of God alone.[49] When Gaismair referred to the Mass as an abomination he is using a word which Zwingli used for it.[50]

But again it would be wrong to assume that Gaismair simply uncritically copied from Zwingli. We remember that church functions had totally ceased in Brixen in midsummer of 1525 and that already then Gaismair had called in evangelical clergy. Gaismair's rejection of the Roman cult at that time was likely motivated not by doctrinal but by social considerations. For the Mass was at the centre of the

---

[48] *Macek III*, 131.
[49] *ZSW* II, 656.
[50] *Ibid.*, 660.

power of the clergy over the people. The priest held the key to heaven for everyone, and many a priest was aware of the advantage that held for him. Many clergy charged fees for the spiritual ministrations which only they could perform so that church rites became a source of oppression on the common man. As stated earlier, anything that was contrary to justice and mercy was, according to Gaismair, contrary to God and thereby already stood condemned. Again therefore one may be justified in assuming that Zwingli's views provided Gaismair with a systematic justification for removing what he had already rejected on other grounds.

Article seven then deals with the preaching of God's Word which is to take the place of the rejected Roman cult with its appurtenances. Such preaching is to be faithful to the truth, concentrating on the Scriptures. All argument proceeding from human wisdom and which therefore does not have its source in Scripture, and all appeal to church law or any other rule than that of Scripture is to be rooted out. And to insure that it will not again cause confusion the books of theology and canon law which in the Roman church have virtually replaced Scripture are to be burned. Particularly this last provision, for which the only known Reformation precedent is the burning of the books of canon law by Luther and his students in December 1520, shows how serious Gaismair was about the faithful preaching of God's Word. Undoubtedly Gaismair was also aware of the Catholic practice of burning what were considered pernicious books. This included popular translations of the Bible. On May 4, 1515, Leo X issued an order that all forbidden books were to be burned. The church based itself specifically on Acts 19:19.[51] Gaismair was thus perhaps simply advocating what was customary except that now the roles were reversed. The character and functioning of his envisaged state is determined by the faithful preaching of God's Word, and no remnants of the old exploitive order are to be left which might endanger it. As was the case with both Luther and Zwingli, a tremendous burden is placed on such faithful preaching of God's Word. The Reformers depended on the Word to bring about reform. In Gaismair's case the carrying out of the reform by force was itself justified by the Word, and then the Word would be preached in order to ensure the continuance of the Christian order.

Article eight calls for the creation of parishes according to the

---

[51] Wetzer and Welte *op. cit.*, II, 1437-1444 and *Evangelisches Kirchenlexikon*, Göttingen, 1956, I, 600-602.

greatest convenience in order that all administration may be conducted at the lowest cost possible. Again this provision emphasizes the importance to Gaismair of the preaching of the Word. The urge to provide spiritual guidance to the people at the lowest cost must not be interpreted to imply that it is of minimal importance. It must be seen in the context of the experience of high cost and minimal service characteristic of many parishes in Tyrol under the Roman church because of absenteeism and unqualified and unsuitable vicars. Such abuse of the money which the common people gave to the church was to be done away with.

In section 16 Gaismair discusses briefly the financial basis of the preaching of God's Word. Every parish is to have one priest according to the teaching of Paul, who will proclaim the Word. That and that only is his duty. It is somewhat surprising to see Gaismair use the term priest in view of what that implied to him. Here Gaismair's dependence upon Zwingli is clearly evident. In fact, it is as good as certain that he had at his elbow a copy of Zwingli's *Auslegen und Gründe der Schlussreden*. In the sixty-second article Zwingli wrote that he was ready to allow for priests provided that the term is used in its New Testament sense, namely that a priest is a proclaimer of the Word of God. For this he appeals to the teaching of Paul in Titus 1:5-9 and I Tim. 5:17 and Gaismair faithfully follows him.[52]

The next point concerns the support of the priests. The tithe, which is commanded by God, is to be used for their support. Zwingli deals with this in the sixty-third article, appealing again to Paul who cites the Old Testament precedent of the priests who were supported by the tithe.[53] Gaismair however adds that they are to get honourable support, sufficient to their needs. This too speaks of the importance with which Gaismair invested the role of the preachers. The tithe is a command of God and therefore required, but its use is to be carefully specified. If any tithe is left after the clergy have been well looked after it is to go to the aid of the poor. About this too Zwingli had written, insisting that the tithe should be paid but that the government should see that all abuses relating to its use would be eliminated.[54]

The thirteenth article dealing with the school for the training of preachers has already been discussed above and no more needs to be

---

[52] *ZSW* II, 441. "Also lass ich hie gern priester sin, die by der Kilchen lerend, die, so das gotswort verkundend..."

[53] *Ibid.*, 441-443; IV, 356-357.

[54] *Ibid.*, II, 512-515.

said about it here except that perhaps no other single provision of the Constitution speaks so strongly of Gaismair's conviction of the importance of God's Word for the new order he envisioned for Tyrol. Let it be said again. The divine imperatives are viewed as the salvation of Tyrol. If the church in its old form was consigned to extinction, the Word of God was to be all the more in evidence. Gaismair's Tyrol was therefore in no sense viewed as a secular state. Its form was rather more like the Old Testament-oriented theocracies of Calvin and the Puritans than like a modern socialist state. Even so concise a document as the Constitution does not obscure that.

A part of the church reform dealt with the disposal of the vast properties of the Roman church. Several articles relate to this. Article 11 deals with the capital city of Tyrol. It is to be Brixen primarily because it is geographically central, but also because there is a whole collection of church buildings there that are well suited to house the government.[55] The buildings which had for so long served the interests of a few were now to serve the common good. The use of the monasteries and the very considerable holdings of the Teutonic Knights especially in Sterzing and Bozen is described in section 17. The buildings are to serve the sick as hospitals, and as homes for the elderly and homeless children. Again, what formerly served the appetites of the few now serves the needs of the many. Section 21 provides for the smelting down of all gold and silver from the churches to be used for the common good. At these points too Zwingli supplied models.[56]

Basically the Constitution is a cry for justice. Almost every article expresses either directly or indirectly, Gaismair's passion for righteousness. His mood is that of the angry and uncompromising Old Testament prophet who went beyond hurling oracles at the feudal powerholders, but set about to do away with the "countless sacrifices," "the sacred seasons and ceremonies," the "festivals," the "countless prayers." He saw clearly the blood on the hands of the powerful and concluded with the prophets that God had rejected the worship of such men. He now took it upon himself to "pursue justice and champion the oppressed; give the orphan his rights, plead the widow's cause." In his vision he saw justice rolling on "like a river

---

[55] There were primarily the bishop's castle and the houses of the cathedral canons.

[56] This will be discussed in detail below.

and righteousness like an ever flowing stream." [57] His concern for
social justice is not rooted in a rational renaissance humanism but
in the biblical tradition as we have tried to show. It is therefore altogether an expression of Gaismair's religious faith. In fact social
justice is equated by Gaismair with the true and only valid expression
of that faith.

In article 2 the persecution of the eternal Word of God is practically equated with the oppression of the common man and the frustration of the common good. The fourth article also deals with this basic
issue. All special privileges are to be abolished. It is to be done because special privilege is against God's Word since it perverts justice
and is itself a perversion of justice. By implication Gaismair here
broaches the principle of the equality of all men. We know from his
own mouth that he actually intended to do away with the clergy, the
nobility, and even with the well-to-do burghers of the towns. Insistence upon and fighting for special privilege of wealth, social
status, and legal advantage would for Gaismair be "persecution of
the Word of God."

Gaismair dramatically shows his determination to assure equality
in article 5 which provides for the total destruction of city walls and
all fortresses which exist for the sole purpose of separating some
citizens from others. Only villages are to be left, meaning not that
the cities themselves are to be destroyed,[58] but that the cities shall be
like villages in that they have no special protection not enjoyed by
all others. This is to ensure that no person is more privileged or
considered better than any other. There is to be absolute equality
throughout the whole land. The germanic ideal of equality which
had been a mainstay of peasant movements prior to the Reformation
was united in Gaismair with the Reformation emphasis on the worth
and freedom of the individual into one of the foundation stones of
his vision. Special privileges and social differences between men are
the root of social disintegration, tyranny, and rebellion. In order to
assure social peace and welfare all social distinctions will have to be
abolished.

Articles eight to thirteen deal directly with the safeguarding of the

---

[57] Isa. 1:10-17; Amos 5:21-24.
[58] *Macek I*, 370, interprets this article to call for the destruction of the cities
themselves. That this cannot be so is indicated by the fact that Brixen, with its
clerical buildings is to serve as capital, and Trent because of its location as the
industrial centre.

legal process. There shall be justice equally available to all without fear or favour. Gaismair had seen the arbitrary nature of justice as applied to the poor and also to himself. First of all the jurisdictional units (*Gerichte*) will be determined by the rules of convenience and accessibility so that justice can be given at minimal cost (art. 8). No longer will they have to go long distances at great expense but justice will be given at home where people and their circumstances are known. All the people in every jurisdiction will annually choose one magistrate and eight jurors who will perform all judicial functions for that year (art. 9). This would deliver them from the professional jurists as well as from the disadvantage of magistrates who were strangers, having received the appointment as a favour. Judgement will be given by their peers who are themselves subject to the same kind of judgement. The period of a year will give judge and jury time to get acquainted with their tasks but will be short enough to prevent the development of an entrenched judicial power.

The localization of justice reflects not only the passion to see justice achieved but also the determination to see to the continuance of common law as the law of the land. Thus the legal process will need to be localized and conducted by officers from each local area because of the local nature of common law.

The court will sit every Monday and the cases brought before it are not to be delayed but disposed of within two weeks. This is designed to do away with the interminable delays in getting a judgement. Delays were often deliberate because that provided greater possibility for gain at the expense of the plaintiff and accused. Magistrate, jurors, secretaries, lawyers, messengers, and other judicial appointees will receive a salary plus expenses from the state. Thus they would not be tempted to receive bribes (art. 10). The Appeals will go to the government in Brixen and no longer before the vice-regent at Meran. They too are to be dealt with quickly without delay (art. 11, 12).

Section 14 deals with the question of taxes which, Gaismair says, may have to be paid because funds will likely be needed for military purposes for a while. What is of special importance is that that will be decided by common consultation. There is to be no arbitrary imposition of taxation without consulting the people who have to pay. When taxes are called for they are to be borne equally by the whole land (section 25). In section 17 he suggests that an income tax may be the way to equalize the burden should a tax be required. Duty on goods is to be abolished in Tyrol, for that will contribute to the common good. Imports are to be duty free, but exports are dutiable. This provision was designed to keep especially grain and meat in the country since Tyrol was always short of these staples with consequent high prices (section 15).

Sections 16 and 17 are devoted to the care of the poor and indigent. The tithe is a law of God and therefore will be given to support the preachers and beyond that for the care of the poor. Begging from house to house is to be stopped in order to do away with the social disintegration which accompanies a situation of poverty and unemployment. The houses of the monasteries and the Teutonic Knights are to be turned into social service centres. Hospitals, in which proper care and medical attention is given will be established. Other buildings are to be used for homes for the aged who can no longer work, and yet others for the shelter care of orphan children who are to receive a proper education in order that they become honourable people. The very poor are to receive not merely a subsistence dole but provided with whatever they need. Special officials salaried by the government will administer and be responsible for reporting on the whole aid program. The cost for these services is to be borne by the whole community through tithes, voluntary gifts, and, if these do not suffice, an income tax. No longer is any person to suffer want in Tyrol.

It is to be assumed that Gaismair followed the model he saw in Zürich for the use of church properties, for there the monasteries were dissolved in December, 1524, and put into the service of the community for the care of the sick and indigent. All the moneys which continued to accrue from pious foundations were consigned to a social service fund, and special administrators were appointed to oversee the service.[59] Evidently the system was working and was effective and Gaismair was impressed with it.

Section 18 deals with agriculture, especially with the reclaiming of arable land from the marshlands at Meran and Trent and the production of needed commodities. There should be less wine and more grain and meat. He is concerned to raise the general level of health among the people. The communities are to set aside a convenient

---

[59] O. Farner, *op. cit.*, III, 521-536. Zwingli himself wrote: "Die der geistlich genanten pracht, rychtag und mutwillen darumb beschirmend, das sy ir überschwenckliche rychtag niessend, die aber den armen ghörend, unnd uss den spitälen der armen herbergen der rütern und söldneren machend, das ist: uss den klösteren. Denn die klöster sind nüt anders den spitäl der armen ..." (*ZSW* II, 340).

time once a year when they give proper care to the common pastures, to get rid of weeds and so gradually improve the land (section 19). While the land remains in private hands, Gaismair clearly intends people to understand that with it they may not serve simply their own interests, but the health and welfare of the whole community. These proposals testify to Gaismair's farsightedness in economics. Only the mobilization of the total resources of the community could accomplish such a tasks as the draining of extensive marshlands.

Then Gaismair turns to the commercial sector. No private commercial enterprise is to be allowed since that depends on charging high interest, which is a means of oppression (section 19). It is all to be placed in the hands of the state. Trent is to become the industrial centre for the production of needed commodities such as textiles, shoes and other goods since it lies conveniently on the main trade route and is the port of entry for the goods from Venice and the east.

The goods produced are to be sold at the cost of production in special stores located conveniently throughout the land. Thus prices will be held down, everyone will be assured of quality wares, and, since the profit motive is removed, deception and inflation will be avoided. A salaried government official with a salaried staff will be responsible. While one may not be as convinced as Gaismair seems to have been that this would do away with all abuses, the point to note here is that Gaismair means to do away with high costs to the poor and high profits to the already wealthy (section 19). Its justification is the good of the common man.

This concern also dominates in sections 23 and 24 dealing with the mining enterprise. All mining works and smelteries now held by the nobility and the great banking houses such as the Fuggers, the Hochstetters, and the Baumgartners are to be expropriated and put into the hands of the people. The big companies have forfeited their right to them since they have become wealthy by usury and the shedding of human blood. By concentrating economic power in their hands they have controlled wages and prices, making the former low and the latter high, and oppressed the whole world with their unchristian usury. They have passed sentence on themselves at the bar of divine justice and they are now properly punished and done away with. Again an appointed government official will be the general administrator and will be accountable to the people by annually reporting on the industry. Workers are to be paid proper wage in cash, not in goods in order to assure amicable relations between miners and

the rest of the population.[60] The mines are to provide the income for
the cost of government and for this reason the industry is to be ex-
panded (section 25). That this was an entirely realistic expectation can
be seen from the size of the enterprise.[61] It was because of the rich
income from the mines that Tyrol was referred to as the "treasure
chest of the Emperor." All of that is now to go to the common
good.

In sections 19, and 23-25, Gaismair has plowed virgin soil. There
had for a long time been loud complaints about exploitive commercial
practices and the rapacity of the big companies. As long ago as 1439
the writer of the *Reformatio Sigismundi* had called for the abolition of
the great companies and condemned the practice of artificially induc-
ing inflation by withholding goods in order to drive up the price.[62]
Luther had condemned the commercial oppression [63] and Zwingli
had written strong words against usury and developing capitalism.[64]
But neither Luther nor Zwingli had any intention of seriously inter-
fering with the commercial underpinnings of society. Gaismair, perhaps following the *Reformatio Sigismundi* and encouraged by Zwingli's
strong words, securely builds the abolition of private commercial
enterprise into his vision for the new agrarian republic, and he is
entirely serious about carrying it out. Although Zwingli had written
that private property was a consequence of sin [65] and that a Christian
is only a steward of his property for the benefit of all,[66] his words
were not turned into action. For Gaismair this view of private property is basic; without it his whole vision would vanish.

The passionate thrust for justice which we noticed in the very first
notations from Gaismair's hand, and which characterized his two
protests to the Council in Innsbruck, carries in accelerated momentum
and volume through the Constitution. It is now not merely a cry, but
an appeal to the holders of power to relent and give justice. It is now
harnessed to a social program totally without precedent, which in

---

[60] ". . . dem arbaiter alle raittung mit parem gelt und mit khainem pfenwbert
[sic] hinfuran bezazllung thuen." Tension had long existed between the social
groups because the miners were often paid in kind which, in view of the large
number of miners, meant considerable loss to the community producers of food
goods.

[61] *Macek I*, 10-11.

[62] Koller, *op. cit.*, 274, 314.

[63] R. H. Bainton, *Here I stand: A Life of Martin Luther*, New York, 1950,
236-238.

[64] *ZSW* II, 339-340.

[65] *ZSW* II, 511.

[66] *ZSW* II, 451.

most of its provisions had sufficient concreteness to warrant actual implementation.[67] Gaismair himself was no peasant but a man with extensive legal expertise and an exhaustive knowledge of the land and its strengths and weaknesses. Moreover he provided for other trained people in the government. He envisaged however, an agrarian republic from which the clergy, the nobles and the financial moguls had been expelled, and there is every reason to assume that he saw peasants themselves in leadership roles in the local communities. This expectation is not as utopian as is sometimes assumed by twentieth century technologically minded analysts. It is at least an open question whether in the end the powerful incumbents with their expertise produced a more viable and progressive order than Gaismair's Constitution might have done had it been given an opportunity.

3. DIFFERENCES BETWEEN GAISMAIR AND ZWINGLI

It has been shown above how at many points Gaismair followed Zwingli and the Zürich model in his Constitution. Some further comments on the relationship of Zwingli and Gaismair need now to be made. Oskar Vasella writes that without doubt Gaismair enjoyed a high reputation in Zürich.[68] Alongside this we should consider the following fact. Early in 1525 Zürich had its version of peasant unrest, which the Council and the clergy just managed to control.[69] One of the chief agitators was executed in June as a warning for others. Zwingli addressed a letter to the farmers of Zürich in early June 1525 in which he appealed to them not to make an insurrection and particularly not to allow any outside agitators to deceive them into revolt.[70] By the time Gaismair came to Zürich in October 1525 the comparatively mild peasant disorders had long disappeared. Nevertheless Zürich might have had reason to be wary of so capable a peasant leader as Gaismair, particularly when it was known that he was gathering disaffected peasants for an attack on Tyrol. It may be assumed that Gaismair, in return for help against the Habsburgs

---

[67] But see Franz, *Der Deutsche Bauernkrieg*, 1972, 159, and Allen Dirrim, "Recent Marxist Historiography of the German Peasant's Revolt—A critique," *Bulletin of the Library: Foundation for Reformation Research*, Vol. 4, no. 2 (June, 1969), 23.

[68] Vasella, *op. cit.*, 407.

[69] *ZSW* II, 338-344.

[70] *ZSW* IV, 357. "... so lassend uch mit etwas hargeloffner frömbdlingen die damit underschlouff by uch suchend, noch etlich eygennützig oder verdorben lut wider sy hetzen und unruwigen, das christenem volck gar nit zimpt."

had to promise not to engage in any kind of subversive activity while in Zürich. That the possibility of incitement to revolt still existed in the Zürich countryside can be concluded from the fact that although the removal of serfdom and the small tithe had been proposed by a committee appointed by the city Council in response to peasant demands, in fact the farmers had achieved nothing.[71]

It is also virtually certain that Gaismair would of his own accord not have made any overtures to local dissidents since that would have put an immediate end to any hope for help from Zwingli. Thus the interests of the Zürich peasants, some of whom were worse off than those in Tyrol, had to be sacrificed to the possibility of getting aid from their rulers to liberate peasants elsewhere. An agreement with Zwingli and the Council may also be the reason why Gaismair made no known contact with the Zürich Anabaptists who had formed the first "free" church in Zürich in January 1525. Conrad Grebel was spreading his views in the area while Gaismair was there and, together with Georg Blaurock and Felix Manz, was imprisoned in Zürich on November 18, 1525. Gaismair cannot have been unaware of these events, especially since Grebel's imprisonment was justified by the authorities in part by his participation in peasant unrest in the previous June.[72] But it also seems clear enough that while he certainly had things in common with these Anabaptists, he was not, as they were, interested in a church freed from all ties with the government. He was interested in justice for Tyrol for which he needed military help from Zwingli. Any open association with them would quickly have led to his expulsion from Zürich.

For all of Gaismair's debt to Zwingli there are also basic differences between the two which are extensive enough that it would be misleading to call Gaismair a Zwinglian. Zwingli would never have accepted Gaismair's Constitution had it been proposed as a possibility for Zürich, but would have condemned it as subversive even as he condemned the aspirations of Conrad Grebel and Felix Manz as subversive. For while Gaismair had thrown the gauntlet down to the propertied classes, the nobles and the townspeople, Zwingli was especially interested in getting precisely their support for his movement. It gave status to the evangelical faith and, which was even more important, the needed economic and political support. For the same

---

[71] O. Farner, *op. cit.*, IV, 143.
[72] *Ibid.*, 134-135.

reason also Zwingli made no moves to interfere with the workings
of the great commercial companies, even though he criticized their
practices. By doing so he would have alienated significant segments
of his support. Hence he also defended the paying of interest.[73] A
major point of the Constitution is the prohibition of private commercial transaction. Similarly, Zwingli could not have thought of ex-
propriating the holdings of the big companies which for Gaismair
represented a non-negotiable demand. Although Zwingli insisted that
all men were brothers, he did nothing to remove class distinctions, a
concern that is at the very heart of the Constitution. There is thus an
unbridgeable difference between the two on several basic social
issues.

One is also forced to the conclusion that Gaismair differed from
Zwingli in his view of the reformed faith. As has already been pointed
out, there is no reference to Jesus or to the Reformation principle
of justification by faith. The total avoidance of these matters in all
the material we have about Gaismair even by allusion leads to the
conclusion that they were excluded by design. Gaismair appears to
have been uninterested in the major theological issues disputed in
Reformation times. He had a practical turn of mind which worked
in concrete issues. It was suggested above that in the area of political
theory even the Reformers did not mention Jesus and that this would
in part explain Gaismair's silence about Jesus in the Constitution. It
may also be argued that in the mass of peasant statements references
to Jesus are rare and that therefore Gaismair was simply following
the norm. Nevertheless, it is strange that a man who regarded himself not only as a political theorist but also as reformer never mentions
Jesus or justification by faith either in the Constitution or anywhere
else. Perhaps Jesus was left out because Christian theology had given
him an abstract soteriological function, which, as especially Luther
insisted, had to do with the salvation of the soul. Jesus had, by the
church, been pushed out into the practically inaccessible metaphysical
regions of trinitarian dogma and had been so docetized that a man
like Gaismair, who was concerned about social justice, likely found
the whole matter totally irrelevant to his aims.

The differences between Gaismair and Zwingli are therefore as
substantial as the resemblances. Gaismair clearly depended on Zwingli
for those social and theological views which suited his purpose and
program. He followed Zwingli in his interpretation and use of the

---

[73] *ZSW* II, 515-516.

Old Testament but not of the New. Gaismair's relationship to Zwingli once again demonstrates the man's independence. He was ready to borrow from others what was useful, but was at the same time determined to go his own way.

4. Gaismair and the Anabaptists

Macek makes a good deal of Gaismair's contact with and movement toward Anabaptism. He even suggests that he was a member of the group.[74] We will therefore gather together at this point everything that relates to that part of Gaismair's life and see whether it influenced his thinking in any way.

The first piece of information cited as evidence by Macek comes from Venetian sources dated late in 1526. On December 7, 1526, the mayor of Brescia wrote a letter to the Signoria in Venice in which he reported that Gaismair's wife had given birth to a son. In his elation Gaismair had invited the Rectors of the city to stand godfather for the child. They had declined the request, but had, in the name of the city, presented Mrs. Gaismair with a piece of silk cloth for a dress which had made her very happy. Evidently the Rectors had second thoughts about the refusal since they had come to realize that by acceding to the request Gaismair would have become more than ever indebted to his patrons. The letter stated that they regretted "not to have baptized him." [75] Macek interprets this to mean that Gaismair refused to have the child baptized, and that there was some indignation in Venice because of it.[76] But this appears to be going beyond the evidence. In the first place such an interpretation is possible only if the phrase is lifted out of its context. Secondly, the statement may mean no more than that they declined to participate in the baptism in the requested way. This interpretation is strengthened by the statement of Gaismair's wife in a letter to the Signoria after his death. She writes that the children born to them in Padua were all baptized according to the Roman rite.[77] It is

---

[74] *Macek I*, 472.

[75] Wieser and Schubring, *op. cit.*, 13. The Italian text from Marino Sanuto, *I Diarii*, ed. F. Stefano *et al.*, Venezia, 1899-1904, XLIII, col. 400 reads: "Et in Collegio si dolseno molto ditti rectori non haverlo baptizato, per far ditto Michiel piu sviscerato marchesco."

[76] *Macek I*, 453, 472.

[77] Wieser, *op. cit.*, 26 after Sanuto, *op. cit.*, LVI, 68: "... suos his natos baptzari fecit in templo Sanctae Sophiae cum omnibus cerimoniis quae in sacro baptismate observari solent...."

therefore safe to assume that the child born earlier in Brescia was also baptized, although without the Rectors. One of Macek's main points for connecting Gaismair with the Anabaptists therefore drops away. While it would certainly have been possible for Gaismair to have been influenced by Anabaptists by this time, especially through contacts with the Zürich group, this incident cannot be used as evidence of such influence.

There is, however, definite evidence of contact between the Gaismair movement and the newly developing Anabaptist movement in Tyrol, as well as between Gaismair himself and members of the group. Gaismair knew about them from Zürich when, if he had had any inclination to seek contact with them, he was unable to do so, because he was anxious to preserve cordial relations with Zwingli. Since Anabaptists were religiously and socially considerably more radical than Zwingli we may assume that he would have been concerned to contact them once he became aware of their presence in Tyrol. The fact that he had so far failed to realize his vision for Tyrol would increase his interest in people who were espousing a cause which at a number of points bore striking resemblance to his own vision.

Before we consider the specific instances of contact between Gaismair and the Anabaptists, a review of the main evidence concerning the emergence of the group in Tyrol is called for. Precise dates and names are not available, but scattered bits of evidence indicate that Anabaptism came to Tyrol early from both west and east. On November 14, 1525, Marx Sittich von Ems in Vorarlberg reported to Innsbruck about a preacher who preached against the Mass, the giving of the tithe, and private confession. He also said that both the ecclesiastical as well as the secular authority ought to be done away with. The day for lords is past, since all men are lords. This truth has now been revealed by God and he and others are called to proclaim it.[78] There is no reference to Anabaptism in the letter, but the preacher could have been neither Lutheran nor Zwinglian. This is indicated especially by the rejection of spiritual *and* secular authorities, as also by the claim to revelation and the divine commandment to preach which is entirely characteristic of the Swiss Anabaptists. While we have no clear evidence that this man was an Anabaptist, it is quite possible that he was expressing Anabaptist ideas—although in garbled form—that had come over perhaps from St. Gall where the movement

[78] TLRA *HR 106*, 68. Cf. J. M. Stayer, *Anabaptists and the Sword*, Lawrence, Kansas: Coronado Press, 1972, pp. 107-113.

ran high in the summer of 1525.[79] In addition the letter comes from Vorarlberg and not Tyrol, but it is introduced here because it could represent an early instance of the eastward movement of Anabaptism.

In May of 1526 Kaspar Färber, a native Tyrolian, told Hans Hut in Augsburg that several brothers in the Inn Valley had been baptized and were leading a Christian life[80]. Thus Anabaptists were found in Tyrol early in 1526. It is virtually certain that they became Anabaptist through the efforts of missionaries from Switzerland. Georg Blaurock and Felix Manz worked in Chur mid-May 1525 and a little later Blaurock was in Appenzell. He worked in both the Grisons and Appenzell again in April 1526.[81]

A cowherd named Wolfgang appears to have carried the new movement from the upper Inn Valley into the heart of Tyrol, the area around Brixen. He was born in the Sarn Valley between Bozen and Sterzing and by his own confession made in Brixen on January 16-18, 1527, had spent a year in the upper Inn Valley, mentioning especially Zirl, Inzing, Innsbruck, and Hall as places where he had spent time. He seems to have gotten his instruction in Hall and Innsbruck, and then, early summer 1526 to have come south and preached all along the Eisack and Puster valleys. Although his preaching includes no reference to baptism he comes close to it in the explicit rejection of confirmation, which, he says, God had not instituted. His repeated reference to following Christ, his statement that he based himself upon the Gospels and the epistles of Paul, and that all human laws were to be rejected (the rejection of the spiritual and secular authority) are common Anabaptist motifs.[82] Later that year (1527) several persons who had been among his staunchest supporters in Klausen were specifically arrested as Anabaptists. Their names were Ulrich Müllner, Peter Pinter, and Gilg Pader and his wife.[83]

---

[79] See John H. Yoder, "The Recovery of the Anabaptist Vision," *CONCERN no. 18*, July, 1971, 10.

[80] Urgicht of Hans Hut in C. Meyer, "Zur Geschichte der Wiedertäufer in Oberschwaben," *Zeitschrift des historischen Vereins für Schwaben und Neuburg* I, 1874, 245. "Caspar Ferber ... sey aus dem Intal purtig, sovil vom widertawf geredt und anzaigt, wie ettlich brueder im Intal wern, die sich hetten lassen tawfen und so ain christenlich leben fuerten ...."

[81] *Mennonitisches Lexikon* I, ed. C. Hege and C. Neff, Frankfurt a. M. und Weierhof, 1913, article "Blaurock."

[82] AVB *Rathsprotokoll 1515-1527*, 759-767.

[83] Letter of George of Austria, bishop of Brixen, to Ulrich Wittenbach and Leonhart von Aichach magistrate in Klausen Dec. 24, 1527, AVB, *Bischof Georgen von Österreich Registratur Gemainer Sachen de annis 1527-1530*, Codex XI, 24-25, 93-95.

Their confessions indicated a considerable number of baptized adherents of the new movement in the area.[84] This is confirmed by a communication of the bishop of Brixen to the government in Innsbruck on December 26, 1527.[85] During the year 1527 then, Anabaptism became firmly established in the area which had been the storm centre of the peasant uprising two years earlier.

Anabaptism came into Tyrol also from the east through the labours of Hans Hut. This passionate and successful Franconian Anabaptist had baptized numerous persons in Salzburg, Linz, Gallneukirchen, Eisenstadt, Melk, and Vienna on a missionary journey in the summer of 1527.[86] In the lengthy interrogation before his death Hut also confessed to having sent a missionary named Hennslin into Austria.[87] Hans Hut's work flowed over into Tyrol late 1527 when Leonhard Schiemer of Vöcklabruck, who had been baptized by Oswald Glaidt, a coworker of Hut, came to Rattenberg in November.

But by the time the movement first appeared above ground in the lower Inn and Eisack valleys late in 1527 the authorities had already acted against it. The movement had excited a good deal of official attention early in 1527 when Michael Sattler and a number of other Anabaptists were arrested at Horb in the Black Forest, which then belonged to Austria and came under the purview of the Innsbruck administration.[88] On April 4, 1527, Ferdinand wrote from Olmütz about the "strange sect" which claims that there is another baptism beside that which was "instituted by Christ himself our Saviour according to the holy Gospel." "Such and similar actions lead only to rebellion, bloodshed and the extermination and destruction of all government and honourable estates even more than heretofore." He urges special watchfulness in Tyrol in order to prevent it from entering.[89] On August 20, 1527, followed the first royal decree against the Anabaptists in which the new movement is again associated with revolt and the total destruction of the societal order.[90] Strong penalties are therefore provided for the adherents of the new sect.[91] There is

---

[84] *Ibid.*, 93-95.
[85] TLRA *CD* II, 106v-107.
[86] C. Meyer, *op. cit.*, 226.
[87] *Ibid.*
[88] TLRA *AKM* III, 49-50v.
[89] TLRA *VKM* II, 35v-36.
[90] TLRA *CD* II, 92. A printed copy has been bound into the volume.
[91] *Ibid.* This decree is an excellent example of how out of touch Ferdinand and his advisers were with the realities of life in Tyrol. It was a public decree, designed

no doubt that the authorities viewed the new movement as another form of revolt directly continuous with the peasant revolt, the living symbol of which was Michael Gaismair.

As for specific instances of contact between Gaismair and the Anabaptists and between the two movements, they are few, and that lies mostly in the nature of the problem. The peasants' revolt had been broken with great cruelty, and since then everyone would try in every way possible to erase any association with it for fear of reprisal. Thus many points of contact which would otherwise have been visible are now forever hidden from our sight. But the few explicit references to contact between the two movements and their carriers are sufficient to show that they were by no means completely separate movements.

On April 26, 1527, the Council in Innsbruck wrote to Jacob Trapp in the Vintschgau about a clergyman sent there by Gaismair to help keep the fires of opposition against Ferdinand burning. There is also reference to a second one named Andre who was with Gaismair, and who now belongs to the "new sect." The term "new sect" here almost certainly means Anabaptism, for it had, as we saw above, gotten into official correspondence for the first time that month.[92] This Andre was earlier a priest in Lüsen, had been in Gaismair's service as a preacher,[93] and had taken part especially in the revolutionary events around Trent in August, 1525.[94] Since, however, the communication to Trapp does not specify what the man preaches there is no way of confirming his Anabaptist views. It is also virtually impossible to trace him in the movement since only his first name is given. The relative care exercised by Innsbruck involving charges of being Anabaptist however makes it fairly certain that we have here the case of a connecting link between the two movements.

Another case of associating the two movements occurs in a letter

---

to be read and posted for everyone to see and read. It is longwinded, involved, and as far as the prescribed penalties are concerned, quite ambiguous. According to a verbal communication to me by Dr. Grete Mecenseffy, the decree was likely prepared by Ferdinand's theological adviser, Dr. Johann Fabri, one of the most hated men in Tyrol. That the decree was virtually unintelligible is shown by a letter of the Council to Ferdinand of Feb. 8, 1528, in which the confusion of the decree is seen to be working in favour of the Anabaptists (TLRA *AKM* III, 151v-155v).

[92] TLRA *CD* II, 17v-18.
[93] TLRA *TE*, 563-567v.
[94] *Macek I*, 314.

of George of Austria, bishop of Brixen, on December 23, 1527.[95] Agitators have come over from Venice into Tyrol among whom are some of Gaismair's men, in order to foment a new revolt. Among them there are reportedly also some belonging to the new sect of Anabaptism who preach in secret places. It may be argued that this is unlikely because of the Anabaptist position of nonviolence. However at this early stage that is not necessarily convincing. When in the case of Wolfgang, the cowherd preacher, a priest in Klausen warned him to leave the area, a farmer named Messerschmidt wrote a threatening letter to the priest and fastened it to the church door. He and Gilg Pader, who were later arrested as Anabaptists, stated that if the priests interfered with him they would beat the priests, which is hardly a nonviolent stance.[96] An association of Gaismair followers with the Anabaptists is therefore quite possible before the strong leadership of people like Hutter firmly fixed the nonviolent posture of Anabaptism.

On February 17, 1528, Ferdinand refers in a letter to the arrest of several persons for Anabaptist activities among which are a man named Gasser and his wife.[87] He is probably one of the Gassers from Pinzagen near Brixen. This man and his wife are clearly stated to have been principals in the recent peasant uprisings. The name appears several times in the lists of prominent Gaismair supporters during the events around Brixen in May and June 1525.[98] The letter also contains the comment that "the intention of Anabaptism is not only the abuse and heretical nature in and of itself but rather for most people unquestionably to make a conspiracy..."

In the cases of Müllner, Messerschmidt, Pader, Pinter, and Gasser we may well have individuals who, after support for or direct participation in the peasant revolt turned their dissent against church and feudal authority into Anabaptism where the resistance to the traditional authorities was at least as strong, although it was nonviolent in nature. It offered a way of actively continuing in a resisting attitude.

On February 23, 1528, the government in Innsbruck informed the authorities in the Vintschgau that Gaismair had had a meeting with a

---

[95] AVB *Registratur Gemainer Sachen*, 23-24. "Es sollen auch etlich darundter sein so von der newen Seckt vnd dem widertauff jn winckheln predigen sollen..."
[96] AVB *Rathsprotokoll*, 762.
[97] TLRA *VKM* II, 145v.
[98] ASB *Cassa 38*, 14F.

number of Anabaptists in the Münster Valley. The purpose of the meeting is stated as being the formation of a conspiracy and understanding to create dissension in the land. Now the regents say that they doubt this, but the fact is that many of the apostate Anabaptists are fleeing into the Münster Valley to seek shelter there or in the Engadine or the Grisons, and that Gaismair had wide support in these areas and carries on his conspiracy there. It is therefore important to find out what their mutual intentions are.[99]

While the Innsbruck authorities doubted that Gaismair and the Anabaptists were making common cause we have no reason to dismiss the report, for there was a considerable area of agreement between Gaismair's views as they have been described above, and those of the Anabaptists.

The case of the letter of Conrad Grebel and his friends to Thomas Müntzer could serve as a parallel here. They wrote to him in the hope that they could make common cause with him even while they criticized his espousal of violence.[100] First of all they agreed with Gaismair on the rejection of the claims to absolute spiritual authority made by the Roman church. Both were uncompromising on that point and came to their rejection of the claim at least in part on identical grounds. These were that the church had forsaken the Word of God and become its own authority, and that its claim to exercising the authority of Christ was cancelled out by its un-Christlike actions. Secondly they agreed that no cleric should hold secular power since it was out of keeping with their primary role of spiritual authority. The fact that Anabaptists went further to say that no Christian should hold the magisterial office need not, at this time, have prevented agreement on other issues. Thirdly, they both rejected the absolutist claims of the secular power, specifically of Ferdinand and his regents, to absolute power over its subjects, although they came at the question from different directions. Gaismair had rejected the government of Tyrol because it was dedicated to pursue its course of oppression against the people. Anabaptists did not reject Ferdinand as sovereign, but denied that he had any right to oppress his subjects, especially by religious persecution, and announced the coming judgement of God on him. Fourthly, both had a powerful sense of justice. God demanded of men to be just and merciful. Speculative theology and

---

[99] TLRA *Buch Tirol* II, 16.

[100] *Spiritual and Anabaptist Writers*, ed. G. H. Williams and A. M. Mergal, Philadelphia: Westminster, pp. 73-85.

glorious liturgy were of less importance than love and mercy and justice, yes, were an abomination before God because they had become means of oppression. They would, fifthly, have agreed on their view of private property as being there not for personal indulgence but for the common good and to be freely shared, on the rejection of exploitive commercial practices, and that the poor should be adequately provided for. Finally they agreed that the old order had to be swept away immediately without compromise so that the new could no longer be corrupted by the remnants of the old order. They differed, to be sure, on the manner of disposing of the old. Anabaptists simply left the ultimate removal up to God in the meantime establishing new forms of community and community governance. Gaismair took the position of his fellow-revolutionary Thomas Müntzer which was to destroy all the godless with the sword.[101]

This represents agreement on some truly formidable issues. Since Gaismair was constantly concerned about the degree of support he could count on in Tyrol when he invaded, we may be sure that he was interested in nurturing contact with people who kept resistance to spiritual and secular tyranny alive through their network of conventicles. Even if they would not support him to the extent of participating in the violent extermination of the clergy and the nobility, they would still represent support in that they would not resist him. While we have only this one specific report of a meeting between Gaismair and Anabaptists, it may be assumed that contacts between the movement continued.

A special case is Friedrich Brandenburger. He was a native of Cologne, was with Gaismair's force during the turbulent days of May and June 1525,[102] and later during 1531-1532 was a travelling companion of the most noted Tyrolian Anabaptist leader, Jacob Hutter.[103] He was arrested, and during his interrogation admitted to having been a soldier with Michael Gaismair. He said that he had been appointed by Gaismair and five others to capture or assassinate Christopher Herbst,[104] the royal administrator at Toblach and Welsberg. He implicated others who he said were also with Gaismair,[105] although there seems to be some doubt as to the truth of some of his accusations.

---

[101] W. Klaassen, "The Nature of the Anabaptist Protest," *Mennonite Quarterly Review*, XLV (Oct. 1971), 304-310.
[102] Weber, *Die Stadt Bozen*, 97; TLRA *CD* IV, 53.
[103] TLRA *CD* IV, 51-55.
[104] TLRA *CD* IV, 53-54.
[105] *Ibid.*, 51-55.

What is certain is that a former Gaismair aide was later aide to a prominent Anabaptist leader. Brandenburger was burned at the stake as an Anabaptist in Toblach in 1533.[106]

Another person who represents a bridge between the peasant movement and Anabaptism was Hans Vischer. He was mentioned above as one of the preachers Gaismair brought into Tyrol in 1525, and is almost certainly identical with Hans Bünderlin, later Anabaptist leader and spiritualizer.[107] Vischer was educated at Vienna and had been a Dominican.[108] He had been released from his monastic vow by "a cardinal",[109] perhaps because he had become interested in the new faith. Where this happened is not known.

During his days at Sterzing he appears to have made repeated inflammatory statements about the authorities, advising the people to throw off the yoke of the nobility as they had done in Switzerland. During his interrogation he tried to soften the charges of fomenting insurrection made against him by saying that he had said such things about foreign authorities only, but had chastised local dissidents for their rebellion.[110]

He appears to have been especially interested in the Zwinglian variety of the new faith since he attended the Baden Disputation in May-June 1526. He must have gone there immediately after his expulsion from Sterzing which took place on 27 April, 1526.[111] From there, for reasons we do not know, he journeyed to Augsburg where he came in contact with Hans Denck. It was here that he joined the Anabaptist movement through baptism.[112] From Augsburg he went back to his home town of Linz where he became the leader of an Anabaptist conventicle while at the same time acting as secretary to

---

[106] TLRA *CD* IV, 91-2.

[107] Grete Mecenseffy, *Quellen zur Geschichte der Täufer: Österreich* I. Teil, Gütersloh: Verlagshaus Gerd Mohn, 1964, 218, footnote 4. Hereafter referred to as *QGT Österreich I*. Manfred Krebs u. Hans G. Rott, *Quellen zur Geschichte der Täufer: Elsass I.*, Gütersloh: Verlaghaus Gerd Mohn, 1959, 232. Hereafter referred to as *QGT Elsass I*. See also J. Loserth, *Pilgram Marbeck's Antwort auf Kaspar Schwenckfelds Beurteilung des Buches der Bundesbezeugung von 1542*, Wien u. Leipzig: Carl Fromme, 1929, 149.

[108] Günther Franz, *Der Deutsche Bauernkrieg: Aktenband*, Darmstadt: Wissenschaftliche Buchgesellschaft, 1968, 336. Hereafter referred to as Franz II. Vischer is referred to as "brueder Hans Vischer," a common identification for a monastic, *QGT Österreich I*, 128, footnote 4).

[109] Franz II, 337.

[110] *Ibid.*, 336-7.

[111] *Ibid.*, 337.

[112] *QGT: Elsass I*, 232.

the nobleman Bartholomäus von Starhemberg. After this he spent some time with Leonhard von Liechtenstein, presumably as a supporter of Hubmaier.[113] Later, however, he moved to a spiritualizing position, likely as a result of his contacts with Denck.

In the cases of Brandenburger and Vischer-Bünderlin it is now impossible to link the resistance of their peasant revolt period in any particular to their Anabaptist resistance. They may therefore be regarded as specific individuals who had concluded that non-violent resistance was a more effective form of resistance to tyranny than violence. As well, it had a firm biblical warrant.

An attempt to find further points of contact between the peasant resistance headed by Gaismair and Anabaptism by comparing lists of participants of the movements proved entirely fruitless. The archival materials yielded a list of 113 specific names of Gaismair supporters. This list was compared with a large list of Anabaptist names prepared by Eduard Widmoser as an appendix to his work on Anabaptism in Tyrol.[114] While there were some identical names in both lists nothing could be concluded from this for they were usually very common names. In a number of cases only the first or else the last name was available. The only name in both lists which is clearly identical is that of Friedrich Brandenburger and a probable duplicate is that of (Hans?) Gasser and his wife about whom we are otherwise informed. There seems very little likelihood that more definite evidence is available since both movements lived and flourished underground.

It has also been suggested that Gaismair was close to Anabaptism because members of his family belonged to the movement. It is true that a number of the Gaismair clan were Anabaptists, but they were cousins, uncles, and nephews [115] rather than brothers or even sons as has been suggested. Little or nothing can be deduced from this for Gaismair's own sympathies.

The clear evidence for contact between Gaismair and Anabaptism is therefore very meagre, and no specific conclusions can be drawn from it for Gaismair's own views. Certainly there is no ground for Macek's unqualified assertion that he likely belonged to the group. It is highly unlikely because of his dedication to the violent overthrow

---

[113] *Ibid.*, 229.

[114] Eduard Widmoser, "Das Tiroler Täufertum," *Tiroler Heimat*, Bd. 16 (1952), 110-128.

[115] See Auckenthaler, "Michael Gaismair's Heimat und Sippe," *Der Schlern* 21, 1947, 18-19.

of the feudal order in Tyrol. In any case, Macek offers no conclusive evidence for his assertion, but only a general association of Anabaptism with what he calls *Volksketzerei* (popular heresy) and Gaismair's sympathies with that.

It is however, possible to draw some broader conclusions about the relationship of the two movements to each other, and then to turn again to Gaismair's personal views. It appears that the judgement of Ferdinand and his advisers and latterly of Macek and others that Anabaptism was the defiant continuation of resistance to the religio-social feudal order that had been crushed in its violent form in the peasant's revolt, is quite likely correct.[116] There is first of all the startling fact that the first clear evidence of Anabaptist activity in Tyrol comes in the fall of 1526. In early July 1526, the last peasant resistance was crushed in Salzburg, and Gaismair and his army fled through Tyrol to Venice. After the first clear evidences of Anabaptist activity in South Tyrol in November and December the movement rose meteorically. Within a year Anabaptists are found all over Tyrol in considerable numbers.[117] There were major concentrations in the Schwaz-Rattenberg-Kitzbühel area where the miners were especially strongly represented, and in the Eisack and Puster valleys. The lower Inn Valley group grew especially because of the influx of missionaries appointed by Hans Hut, but in the Eisack and Puster valleys, the areas of largest concentration, the movement appears to have grown largely from within at the beginning, later being guided and strengthened by outside leaders. We see thus that it was strongest in the area in which the peasant revolt started, and it was here that it held the longest. The failure of armed revolt under so capable a man as Gaismair was probably interpreted by the peasants to be a sign that that form of resistance was contrary to God's will. They had seen their cause as the cause of the Word of God. Therefore it could not fail. When it did fail, rethinking had to be done. At that point the new movement presented itself, a movement acknowledging the rightness

---

[116] See notes 70 and 71 above. *Macek I*, 470. See also Brendler, *Das Täuferreich zu Münster 1534-1535*, Berlin, 1966, 75. He writes: "Dem ideellen Gehalt und der historischen stellung nach ist es [das Täufertum] die Resignations—und Trotzgestalt der frühbürgerlichen Revolution." See further Bücking, *op. cit.*, 134, Franz, *Der Deutsche Bauernkrieg*, 1933, 479, and O. Farner, *op. cit.*, IV, 1960, 145 who says the same thing for the canton of Zürich. For another view see G. Bauer, *Anfänge täuferischer Gemeindebildungen in Franken*, Nürnberg: Selbstverlag des Vereins für bayerische Kirchengeschichte, 1966, 176-177.

[117] This is visible especially in TLRA *CD II, 1527-1529* which contains hundreds of communications about Anabaptists for the years 1528-1529.

of peasant grievances and aims, but proposing a different mode of resistance. It consisted of forming a new Christian community which saw itself as the restitution of the church of the New Testament, in which the old authorities were rejected and turned over to the sure judgement of God. For its internal life it needed no government at all, and in its mutual aid it simply bypassed and condemned the commercial enterprise and the newly developing capitalism. As for the church, Anabaptism regarded the church buildings as temples of idols and what went on inside as an abomination. They were more radical than Gaismair in that they refused to rebaptize the old in any form, choosing to nurture their community life in new ways. They rejected the tutelage of the church by insisting that only adults should be baptized after a personally responsible decision to walk in the footsteps of Christ, and located the present activity of God not in the miracle of changing wine into blood on the altar but in the miracle of changing old human lives into new ones and creating a community where before there had been none. It gave the protest movement a tremendous sense of identity which not even the most draconian Ferdinandian measures could break. It is therefore also not surprising that from the middle of 1526 onwards the evangelical clerics gradually disappear from the scene. They had done much to convince the peasants of the necessity of armed revolt but seem after Gaismair's flight to have lost credit with the people.[118]

Thus we conclude that although Gaismair had contact with Anabaptists and held some views in common with them there were also major differences between them. Gaismair's revolution and Anabaptism did not merge and Gaismair himself was not an Anabaptist.

5. GAISMAIR'S NONCONFORMITY

There are some final testimonies to Gaismair's religious attitudes from the last two years of his life. Some time between March and August, 1530, there was a move in the Venetian Signoria to discontinue Gaismair's annual pension of three hundred ducats given him for faithful service to the Republic. The reason was evidently that they were doubtful of his religious loyalty. In fact one member went so far as to urge that he be brought before an inquisitor to see whether he was perhaps a "Lutheran." A letter from Priamo da Leze, a high official in Padua, was introduced as evidence. This man wrote that

[118] K. Sinzinger, *op. cit.*, 69.

Gaismair had brought him a German Lutheran book with the comment that it was an excellent book and that he would have it translated into Italian and make him a present of it. Da Leze then added that as soon as he got the book he would send it to the Signoria.[119] On August 5, the Signoria wrote to da Leze in Padua to begin an unobtrusive investigation of Gaismair's religious trip to Switzerland and what he did there. He is also to try to get him to translate the book he had spoken of. Then da Leze is to read it so that he can report on it. He is further to find out whether Gaismair has the smell of heresy about him or holds Lutheran views. All his contacts with others are to be watched and a special point is made of finding out about the place where Gaismair regularly goes when he leaves Padua. Finally he is to find out whether any other Germans or persons with Lutheran sympathies are with him. All of this is to be done secretly.[120] While Gaismair's pension was saved by the intervention of friends who pleaded and proved the value and faithfulness of his services to Venice, the suspicions of the Signoria were not removed.

In these communications the word "Lutheran" is generally used for any non-catholic views, since there was a general lack of clarity in Venetia about the distinctions between the various Reformation viewpoints. The book was referred to as Lutheran and therefore we have no way of being certain what it was. It was probably Zwinglian, but could also have been Anabaptist since by 1530 a number of Anabaptist books were circulating, notably those by Balthasar Hubmaier and Hans Denck.

On the other hand a distinction seems to be made in the letter between heretical and Lutheran views. Since the writers were Catholic and since heresy in the Alpine areas was usually connected with the Waldensians, it may be that we have here a faint hint of a suspicion that Gaismair was something else than Lutheran, perhaps more related to the medieval heresies. If that line of argument is legitimate, then we have a possible indication of Anabaptist sympathies, since Anabaptism bore a striking resemblance to Waldensian beliefs at a number of points. Another point in the letter to da Leze is the information that he regularly went to some place outside of Padua.

---

[119] Wieser, *op. cit.*, 5 from Sanuto, *Diarii* LIII, col. 400-401.

[120] *Ibid.*, 74-75. Wieser documents this letter as being in Section 2 of the Secret Letters of the Chairmen of the Council of Ten (1530-31) in the Royal State Archives of Venice. It is a letter that Macek appears not to have used since he makes no reference to it.

Was he attending meetings of some kind, connected with his views? That seems to be the inference of the writer. None of these individual factors proves anything about Gaismair's views. Together they point merely towards the possibility of a radical position on Gaismair's part that went beyond the Reformers, perhaps associated with Anabaptism. It appears as though these ideas ripened in Gaismair only after he went into Venetian exile.[121]

The last witness to Gaismair's religious views and attitudes comes from a grief-stricken letter which his wife, Magdalena, wrote to the Signoria on April 16, 1532, the day after Gaismair's death.[122] She complained that she was completely forsaken by everyone and could get no help from anyone in Padua. The urgent crisis was that the local clergy had refused to give her husband proper burial, and in spite of repeated attempts to find others who would intercede for her or help her she was entirely unable to find anyone. The reason given for the clerical refusal was that Gaismair was accused of being a heretic and was therefore not worthy of Christian burial. Macek asserts that the local authorities were friendly and respectful of Gaismair and bases himself on the fact that in the letter of the mayor of Padua to the Signoria announcing Gaismair's death Gaismair is always referred to as "domino Michiel," the equivalent of the German "Herr," a title of respect.[123] That is accurate enough, and it is therefore doubly strange that when Magdalena Gaismair needed help at this crucial point she had to write to the Signoria in Venice. Something had happened during the course of April 15/16 which made even the mayor of Padua wash his hands of Gaismair. The reason is very likely that the local clergy threatened to make public that the Paduan officials had been harboring a heretic. It is possible that the investigation ordered in 1530 by the Signoria had revealed that their suspicions were justified, but that somehow no report had been made to Venice, or at least that the report that was submitted was friendly to Gaismair.

Magdalena's description of Gaismair's religious activities also reveals the marks of unorthodox religious behaviour. He was, she states in her letter, a pious and godfearing man second to none, and this is proved primarily by appeal to his eager study of the Bible in various

---

[121] See Aldo Stella, *Dall'Anabattismo al Socinianesimo nel Cenquecento Veneto*, Padua, 1967, and H. A. DeWind's review of this work in *MQR* XLV (Jan. 1971), 100.

[122] Wieser, *op. cit.*, 24-27 from Sanuto, *Diarii* LVI, 67-68.

[123] *Macek I*, 483.

translations, and perhaps even of teaching it to his household. She also admits that he never went to church. These assertions unquestionably point to nonconformism. Her explanation that he avoided going out because his life was constantly in danger is undoubtedly correct and therefore an excellent excuse to be offered in place of the real reason which was that he rejected all that the old church stood for. The tone of the letter further leads one to suspect that it may well have been Magdalena Gaismair, the faithful but tired wife, who persuaded her husband to do at least token allegiance to the church by having the children baptized in St. Sophia's church, and having those that died there buried according to the rites of the church. Such urging on her part would be entirely understandable in view of the fact that his existence was hazardous enough without also antagonizing the powerful church, now everywhere on the lookout for heresy. We do not know whether Gaismair was buried in unhallowed ground or whether the Signoria once more honoured its faithful servant. What is clear from the very end of the letter is that Magdalena Gaismair was one with her husband in his views. God, she writes, has appointed you to protect the widows and orphans. It is the government's obligation to grant justice to the weak, regardless of all other considerations.

Gaismair's widow and only surviving son later lived in Zürich from where they attempted to regain some of the confiscated family property. The letter with which this study begins, stated that Gaismair was dispossessed because he had changed his religion. While that was not in fact the immediate reason, in a very real sense it was true. A deliberate return to biblical religion helped inspire Gaismair to become a social revolutionary and reformer.

CHAPTER THREE

CONCLUSION

Michael Gaismair has thus been shown to be a man of considerable stature in the spectrum of sixteenth century leaders. Not only was he a military leader of great ability, but he was also a diplomat, a judicial and political theorist, and a reformer even though he was never able to translate his conception of a unitary religio-social agrarian republic into reality.

Our major problem in trying to bring this man back to life is the paucity of materials about him and especially those relating to the development of his thought. The most obvious gap is that of his early life from his birth to his election as leader in 1525. The fact that we can only extrapolate from the few clues we have in the early years and reason back into the earlier period from the later represents a weakness in present Gaismair research. Nevertheless the reconstruction attempted here upon the meagre evidence cannot be far from the truth considering the man revealed in action and writing in 1525 to 1526.

Sorting out Gaismair's social and religious convictions is difficult even on the basis of the sources we do have when we remember that we have from his hand only three letters and the Constitution. The Constitution itself is very concise, Gaismair apparently having excluded many details which would have been included had it been written under more peaceful conditions.

For the period from January 1526 onward it is further complicated by Gaismair's alliances with Zürich and the Republic of Venice. The alliance with Zwingli necessitated great caution in expressing any views that would have gone beyond the Reformer, perhaps in the direction of a radicalism closer to Anabaptism. This must have been true even of the Constitution, written as it was to be the program of an invading army in alliance with the Zürich Reformer. Gaismair's efforts to build an alliance with Zürich until 1530 prevented any more radical views from emerging to the light of day. They remained unknown although the supposition that he held such views about 1530 has some support. To achieve his ends Gaismair had to make some weighty compromises.

Certainly his residence in the Venetian Republic and the pension he drew there made silence about his views necessary. Without the permission of residence there he would have lost his asylum, his property, and his pension without which he could not live. Many factors therefore conspired to seal the man's lips and prevented him from acting as he might have wanted to.

That his political thought was ahead of his time requires no argument. There is no parallel in the sixteenth century for its radicalism in calling for the sweeping away of the whole ancient order. Not even Cromwell was prepared to do that. We next encounter that spirit most dramatically in the French revolution.

Gaismair's Constitution has been referred to as a utopia, it appears, because he was never able to put his vision into practice. Certainly it cannot be called a utopia if measured by a classic utopia like that of Thomas More. Gaismair's Tyrol was not a "noplace"; it was a possibility. It could have been instituted because it dealt with a real country, real people, and the realities of political life. Some of its provisions had been realized in Zürich, and all of them were to be realized in the future in the democratic and socialist systems of the West. Certainly the course of a republic of the kind Gaismair envisaged in Tyrol would not have been easy and it was not without reason that he provided for a tax for the eventuality of continuing war. Undoubtedly also the Swiss Confederacy in its successful war of independence and its continuing effective resistance to Habsburg ambition was the prime example which gave Gaismair hope and the assurance that another Alpine republic could achieve and maintain independence.

Religiously Gaismair is similarly out of joint with the times. None of the common labels of the time, Catholic, Protestant, or Anabaptist describes him. During his time as a national and international figure he never formally identified with any Christian movement. His views were formed chiefly by what appears to have been a direct exposure to the Old Testament prophetic tradition. This influenced his evaluation and interpretation of the social phenomena of his time and homeland, and these in turn also informed his reading of Scripture. Martin Luther influenced him only slightly. Huldreich Zwingli, on the other hand, influenced him strongly at some points, especially by supplying his practical program with a theological base and likely helping thereby to form it, and by offering practical models for reform. And finally, it may be that Anabaptism also influenced him in his later years. On this last claim the greatest caution needs to be observed.

Where then can we locate Gaismair in the socio-religious spectrum of the sixteenth century? The common labels of that time are not accurate for him. He must therefore be placed in that many-coloured collection of solitary figures in which the sixteenth century abounded among which was Sebastian Franck, Michael Servetus, and Thomas Müntzer, all of whom developed religio-social syntheses of their own and who therefore joined no group. Somehow this magnifies the man. To remain independent in an age of enforced conformity required special resources and strength of character.

Gaismair was outstanding in the military and legal fields, was an original political and social theorist, and an unusual religious nonconformist. Still, while recent research has brought his outlines into clearer focus, much that was Gaismair still eludes us. But even what we know about him makes him one of the significant figures of the sixteenth century.

APPENDIX ONE

THE LETTERS AND THE CONSTITUTION
OF MICHAEL GAISMAIR

1. Letter to Bishop Sebastian Sprentz
June 19, 1525*

Right reverend prince, gracious lord. I am always first your obedient and willing servant, gracious lord. Your lordship may be displeased with me because I left the service of your grace and joined the peasants since your grace has not written to me at all. Hence I am writing your grace this report.

First of all, at the beginning of the revolt there were no more than six or eight armed men who might have made any effective defence of your lordship's castle. Thus I as one person would certainly not have been of any use to your grace either. I am also confident that if your lordship had been here yourself you would have seen that I would not have sustained such harm to my wife, children and position except to your benefit. Thus I have been of more use to your lordship in my present position, for had I not acted so faithfully and decisively, the castle as well as the city would forthwith have been plundered. As soon as I was chosen as leader I ordered that no more plundering should take place and dispersed the people and sent them home again. I established solid order and rule and preserved peace and justice for all. Your lordship's castle has not been harmed except that provisions have been used. No one came into your lordship's rooms until about eight days ago when the committee and I entered to seal your valuables in order to protect them more adequately. I fully intend, God helping me, to act faithfully in all matters in the confidence that no one will be harmed especially since I have the soldiers. However I won't be able to pay or support them much longer, and if they should be dismissed things would be more dangerous than they are now.

May God give us a Christian peace, law and order and be merciful to us, for in my estimation it is the work of God and not of man. In three days this thing spread throughout the land without any con-

---

* Translation based on A. Hollaender, "Michael Gaismairs Landesordnung 1526", *Der Schlern* 13, 1932, 378-379.

spiracy or common purpose: no man would be able to accomplish that in his own strength.

Thus I beg your grace to be patient and sympathetic in these matters, and to commit yourself to God the Lord who never forsakes his own. I would have written your lordship sooner but I was unable to entrust [the letter] to anyone. Your grace will know that I am risking my reputation and my life. I therefore beg you graciously to accept me since I will act faithfully in all things and contribute to peace and tranquility. Please do not increase the risk for me and burn this letter immediately. I would write more but I have no opportunity now. Dated at Brixen on the 19th of June, 1525.

Your lordship's
submissive Michael Gaismair

2. LETTER OF DEFENCE TO THE COUNCIL IN INNSBRUCK, October 9/10, 1525*

Your excellencies, austere, highly learned, noble, firm, honourable, wise, gracious and kind masters. I beg my lords submissively to accept the following statement graciously from a poor man. To begin with, in order that no one charge me with any crime or the breaking of any vow or any wrongdoing, the following are the facts. In the recent revolt in Brixen I joined the townspeople and the peasants, not to injure anyone, but to save the little I had earned by hard work, as indeed several other servants of my lord did after the captain and counsellors of his grace left the castle for safe refuge. After this they chose me for their leader. Immediately on the first day, I dispersed the people and quietly sent them home again. I saved New Abbey and Sagrer, who had also been attacked, the amount of six thousand guilders. I rescued its people, continuously fed the monks and lay brothers, and allowed them to work and bring in the produce according to their need. Further I preserved the castle of my lord of Brixen so that even his steward was never dismissed from his office. While I was still in the castle I saved the convent, the nobility, and all the clergy in the first attack which came before I joined the peasants and became their captain. I negotiated the truce, and faithfully carried out governance and justice to shield and protect, and preserved peace and quiet. I did this at the least possible cost which my lord of Brixen too, had he been there himself, would not have spared.

---

* Translation based on A. Hollaender, "Michael Gaismair's Landesordnung 1526", *Der Schlern* 13, 1932, 381-383.

Then, as soon as His Sovereign Highness took over the administration of the bishopric and appointed a captain, I obligingly surrendered my position and obediently adhered to the truce as you yourselves acknowledged in the letter calling me to Innsbruck. Consequently I was confident that I would be graciously rewarded and paid for such faithful, diligent action, effort, and labour.

Then I received the gracious letter of my lords to come to Innsbruck to report. I obeyed and simply assumed that the intention of my lords was as the letter stated. However the letter was like poison mixed with honey, against which I respectfully protest. For contrary to the amnesty of His Sovereign Highness and the decisions of the Diet I was forcibly arrested.

Secondly, the provost of New Abbey, the clergy of Brixen and Gräfinger have accused me with many lies, and although I have already made sufficient defense on this matter, I will not submit to their charges, but reserve the right to pursue satisfaction.

Thirdly, Doctor Angerer made a demand against me which has been discharged and which was that I, as the lawful authority, took his goods into my care several days after his house had been plundered. Never did I intend unjustifiably to withhold them. He should by rights honour and thank me for this, for had I not been there, he would have lost that too as, according to his complaint, he lost other things. He ought to be grateful because the towns and jurisdictions of the land made no decision about these matters* at the Diet; it remained unwritten. And now it is nevertheless to be done in the absence of the gathering of His Sovereign Highness and the representatives of the people. Indeed, if this is done with everyone in the land it would lead to a new revolt rather than to peace. I do not say this because I am minded to withhold anything from Doctor Angerer, but in my defence as my lords will see in the following concerning Doctor Angerer. He was satisfied with the settling of his first demand. Now, as one of the godless, he has pressed the matter further, attacked me with lies and made charges against me which he can never substantiate. Moreover he has not provided a single proof either in writing or orally that he ever owned or lost the valuables concerned, nor that I took them. Still, my lords had my property impounded at his request against my justified protest. Further impounders partly unlocked, partly broke open my rooms and trunks

---

* Restitution of property taken during the revolt.

and searched all my property contrary to the provisions of the Diet, acting perhaps on your orders or from their own insolence. Thus Angerer's unjust demand was followed by the impounding although he never requested it nor the search of my property, which was adding insult to injury.

Further my wife was so terrified by this violence that both she and the baby she was nursing became ill. Similarly my friends were insolently and threateningly assaulted as though they had become wealthy through me. My wife was wickedly threatened with torture and violence before the magistrate of Sterzing by Kirchmair of New Abbey, in line with the settlement which his lord the provost received from my lords upon his request, in order to get her to testify against me to satisfy his deceitful desire.

Thus I have also been informed of Doctor Angerer's threat that he would not rest until I had been punished, and all as reward for saving his property for him. One can easily conclude that his recent deceitful unjust demand was made simply to rob me and make real his threat, or that he thinks that by doing so he is rid of giving me the proper gratitude and honour which is my due.

Fourthly, the magistrate at Sterzing rejected and refused to accept my bail in contravention of the Decision* so that the settlement favoured Doctor Angerer's desires to excess and I got refusal of bail, searching of my property, and violence upon my person.

Fifthly, in view of my precarious situation I had requested a special order from you to get a deposition from the clergy, who by the decision of the Diet are required to give information, regarding my obedience. This you have denied me and have given me only a *gemain general* according to ancient usage which does not satisfy me.

Sixthly, I have requested permission from my lords to give me leave to gather my own information for my defence since I cannot retain anyone who can adequately do it for me. This too my lords have refused me.

Seventh, I have requested that Doctor Angerer should appear for hearing also under safe conduct in order to ensure equal justice. I have received no reply from my lords.

From all the above I have, firstly, learned enough and received warning that I can expect violence rather than right judgement and have no hope of equal justice. The recent Diet clearly decided that

---

* The settlement of the Diet of 1525.

from now on common and not written law would be binding; it was confirmed by His Highness and he promised to act in accordance with it. Thus against my request and without proof of the charges I have been judged contrary to common law. For it is the law that no one shall be deprived of defence and right without just cause, and that no one shall be molested in his property, marriage, or anything that has been rightfully acquired, and that in the case of debt or similar matters a man be heard and his case rightly investigated and conducted, where he lives. The decision against me is directly contrary to the provisions of the Diet. Before a legal complaint could be lodged my property was impounded. And as though this were not enough my adversary set in motion his own violent inquisition as it pleased him against my protest and in addition had my property searched and thus disregarded the decision of the Diet even when it was right and proper. Thus my adversaries have achieved more with their mendacious and unproved demand and desire by acting contrary to the Decision than I achieved with my legal protest even though every plaintiff, if he hopes to get redress, must prove his charge according to the common law, and where there is no proof there is no case. But I have not been able to benefit from this practice and common usage.

Secondly, since faith has not been kept with me in the summons to make report when I was arrested, nor in the application of common legal usage contrary to which I was charged, nor in protection and defence against illegal force which was used against me, my honour, my wife, my friends, and my property, I cannot be charged with any breaking of promise. Since His Sovereign Highness' favour in the amnesty has been contravened, since I cannot believe the government which is obligated to act in good faith toward me, and can only expect violence instead of justice, I feel entirely justified in my actions. And if none of that applied, the period of detention which was forced upon me has, according to common law, more than expired, and is no longer binding. For it is common usage that, in case of arrest, a man must be brought to trial within a fortnight. If that is not done the detention is null and void. It follows from this that, according to common law, I too am free long since, seeing I was in prison in Innsbruck for seven weeks. Since no one came to press charges I am free of obligation. I therefore defend myself and claim justification in the matter of the charges, the arrest, and the pledge for the sake of my honour. For these reasons and sufficient causes and not because of crime or despising of equal justice I left Innsbruck. I left also because of the unjust impounding of my property contrary to common law, and respectfully request that it be made available to me according to my need and that my request be graciously granted. And since in all things I have respectfully sought to do right according to my ability, and am determined still to do, I submissively beg my lords to grant me an adequate safe conduct to and from the trial. Regardless of the amnesty of His Sovereign Highness—I will not appeal to it to invalidate a judgement—I will appear for trial before incorruptible judges and jurors as it is right and proper.

My lords will also surely bring the provost of New Abbey, Doctor Angerer, the chapter of Brixen and Gräfinger along with all their supporters to justice and ensure that they will remove and make proper amends for the disgrace, violence, and damage inflicted on me, my wife, and my friends by taking the law wickedly into their own hands contrary to justice and propriety, and that they clear me, my wife, and my friends of all charges, and to pursue the claims they profess to have through the court.

Secondly, I request that my lords will graciously relieve me of the costs which I incurred because of the summons to come to Innsbruck.

I expect that my lords will not charge me nor do me any violence nor allow anyone else to do so contrary to the amnesty of His Sovereign Highness. For I acted honestly, faithfully, and well which, I hope to God, everyone will perceive in time. If, however, I am charged by anyone I request my lords to identify him and hear me also. And if in anything that I am not aware of I should have failed, I ask my lords to remember that I am not perfect, and that more knowledgeable people than I have the same experience. I have also occasionally had to act to please the common man so that no disorder develop in the jurisdictions during the truce and new revolt occur, which would have weighed even more heavily to my disadvantage. May my lords therefore not forget my good deeds and remember only to punish the small misdeeds, but to let the first cancel out the second. And if I should have acted wrongfully—of which I am not aware—and cannot benefit from His Sovereign Highness' amnesty, I ask my lords to inform me about it thoroughly and I will adopt the proper attitude. All of this I expect respectfully to gain from my lords. If however this my defence is not accepted and my proper request is denied, I would have cause for further complaint and to seek protection against all unjust violence of the godless monks and priests. Nor do I want to hide from my lords that eighteen towns and jurisdictions along the Eisack have assured me that they will see me unharmed in all that concerns my actions on their behalf or my role in the government. Now I have deliberately and repeatedly avoided calling on them in order that no new revolt develop for I would rather work for tranquility than unrest. But if I should be apprehended or charged again I would have to call on them for protection in my extremity and for my defence, and there is no doubt that they would be as good as their word. And should another revolt develop in this way—for the embers are still glowing—which I do not desire, accept this as my defence. I submit that my lords should graciously consider this.

Your graces' submissive
Michael Gaismair

3. Second Letter of Defence to the Council in Innsbruck, October 25, 1525*

Your excellencies, austere, highly learned, noble, firm, honourable, wise, gracious lords. With this letter I am sending my lords a protest against my adversary. When my lords read it, I beg that you will receive it graciously in view of my extremity, remembering that no one needs to be ashamed to submit his case and defence to a court, nor that anyone should be spared if it rules to his disadvantage. I request that my lords graciously respond to my earlier request so that I can take further steps to act in my need. This I expect to gain from my lords and respectfully commit myself to you. Dated on the 25th day of October, anno, etc. 1525.

Your graces' submissive
Michael Gaismair

My, Michael Gaismair's Protest Against the Provost of New Abbey

To begin with, since the demand of the provost regarding the restitution of goods taken from him concerns the whole community of the towns and jurisdictions along the Eisack and all those related to them in the revolt, who have covenanted with them, be it known that because of the strength of their unity, they may in no way be legally separated. For this reason, according to our union with each other, I neither will nor may be separated from them since I am not their representative nor can I make promises for them. They have given me no right nor order as one man to speak for them all or in

---

* Translated directly from a photocopy of *Autogramm* E15 in the TLRA:

any way to enter into dealings concerning this matter. Inasmuch as the charge concerns me as a single person along with all the others related to me, I will not, on the strength of our covenant, be sundered from them.

Secondly, the return of the seized valuables concerns all the people. Since His Sovereign Highness has pardoned and absolved what is past, and the Diet passed nothing concerning restitution, it remained unwritten. The advantage of that now becomes apparent, namely that the valuables referred to may go to him who judges and decides. Now that His Sovereign Highness has left the land and the peoples' representatives have gone home, no one has the right or authority in their absence to settle or judge in this matter, for no town or jurisdiction in the land has given its representatives or this committee such right or authority. How then can they do it and honourably answer for it to the people? If they should do it they would place an unbearable and destructive guilt on their shoulders. Should one estate—along with the government and the nobility who sit with it, for they are all of the same ilk—in fact claim the right to make such a decision, the following needs to be said. Firstly, the government has not given them alone this right and thus they have no authority to exercise it. Secondly, we may justly be suspicious and refuse such judgement for the following reason: some of them have also sustained loss. Should they then be judges in a case from which they stand to profit? It is quite clear that their judgement would be their gain. For if they grant restitution to the clergy they have also ruled restitution for themselves.

Thirdly, even if that were not the case I have no certain nor equal access to justice. Nor am I able to get an advocate on behalf of my wife, brothers, and friends, who for my sake were hazed, forcibly imprisoned and otherwise molested, so that we could settle the matter peaceably.

I therefore protest herewith that I am not obligated to appear before this court at this time in the absence of my comrades to reply to the charges against me since they have given me no right or direction so to reply and have themselves not been invited to appear. Further, my lords of the government and the committee have no right or authority to give a judgement on this matter in the absence of His Sovereign Highness and the representatives of the people. They are justifiably under suspicion and their judgement is to be rejected. I will not be tried secretly without defence. If, however, I am tried contrary to proper order and with hostility I will not be bound by the illegal and to me dangerous sentence. I am not obligated to obey and submit to its execution.

Similarly I protest again against Doctor Angerer and all my other adversaries and contest their charges.

4. THE "LANDESORDNUNG"*

(This is the constitution which Michael Gaismair prepared in the 1526th year)

First you will solemnly promise and swear to pledge life and possessions to each other, not to forsake one another, and to act in unity and always by mutual decision. You will faithfully obey the authority set over you, and seek in all things not selfish advantage, but *first* the honour of God and after that the common good, so that Almighty God may give us grace and assistance (as he has frequently promised to all who obey his commandments). Of this we may be completely confident since he is wholly true and deceives no one.

Secondly, that you will exterminate and put away all godless people who persecute the eternal word of God, oppress the common man, and frustrate the common good.

Thirdly, that you will set about to erect a wholly Christian order which is based in all things on the holy word of God, and live by it completely.

Fourthly, all special privileges are to be abolished since they are contrary to the word of God and pervert justice. Thus no one will have an advantage over anyone else.

Cities
Fifthly, all city walls, as well as all castles and fortresses in the land are to be broken down, so that there be no more cities but only villages in order that there be no distinctions among men, and that no one consider himself more important or better than anyone else, for from this may flow dissension, arrogance, and rebellion in the whole land. There is to be absolute equality in the land.

Images
Sixthly, all images, crucifixes, chapels which are not parish churches, and the mass are to be done away with in the whole land, since they are an abomination before God and utterly unchristian.

---

* Translation based on A. Hollaender, "Michael Gaismair's Landesordnung 1526", *Der Schlern* 13, 1932, 427-429. The *Landesordnung* is numbered in articles up to 13. From that point on, for purposes of identification, I have numbered the paragraphs.

Seventhly, the word of God is to be preached faithfully and truthfully everywhere in Gaismair's land. All sophistry and legalism is to be rooted out and their books burned.

Eighthly, the judiciary units in the land as well as the parishes are to be determined according to convenience that they may be administered at the lowest possible cost.

Ninthly, every parish in each judiciary unit is to elect a magistrate and eight jurors annually. These will exercise judiciary power for that year.

Tenthly, the court is to sit every Monday and no case is to be extended beyond two weeks, but completed the following week. The magistrates, jurors, secretaries, advocates, and court officials, and messengers, are not to take money from anyone involved in the cases, but are to be salaried by the state. They are to appear for duty every Monday at the proper place at the state's expense.

Eleventh, a government is to be established in the land, Brixen being the most convenient centre for its location, since it has many church buildings and other conveniences and is centrally located. Regents are to be elected from the four quarters of the land and from the mining community.

Twelfth, any appeals are to come immediately before the government and not to Meran which is useless and an unnecessary expense. Any appeal is to be heard forthwith and completed without any objection.

Thirteenth, a university is to be established at the seat of government, where the word of God alone is to be taught. Three learned men from the university, who know the word of God and have much experience in interpreting holy scripture (from which alone the justice of God can be known), are always to be members of the government in order to decide and judge according to the command of God all things that pertain to a Christian people.

[14] *Taxes* Concerning taxes, the whole population is to consider and decide whether they are forthwith to be abolished, or whether a year of remission should be proclaimed according to the law of God, in the meantime collecting taxes for the general need, for it is likely that funds will be needed for a while for defence.

[15] *Toll* Concerning toll charges, I consider it to be to th ecommon good that they be abolished within the land However at the borders they should be maintained with the

provision that imports are toll-free, but exports will be subject to toll.

Concerning the tithe, it is to be given by everyone according to the command of God, and is to be used as follows: every parish is to have a priest according to the teaching of Paul who is to preach the word of God. He is to be honourably supported from the tithe according to his need, and the rest is to be given the [16] poor. The poor are to be cared for in a manner that prevents door to door begging, vagrancy, and the accumulation of able but unemployed people.

The monasteries and the houses of the Teutonic Knights are to be converted into hospitals. Some will be for the sick where together they can be given proper care and medical treatment. Others will accommodate the aged who can no longer work, as well as indigent orphans who can be taught and honourably brought up. The very poor are to be aided according to their circumstances and need from the tithe or alms, according to the judgement of the local magistrate in whose jurisdiction they live [17] and where they are best known. Wherever the tithe is not sufficient for the support of the pastor and the poor, people are to give alms faithfully according to their ability. If there should be need beyond that it is to be completely met from income (or: a full report is to be made of citizens' income [and a tax levied?]). Every hospital is to have a manager, and beyond that a general administrator over all the hospitals and welfare is to be appointed. It will be his duty to supply the hospitals regularly with whatever they need, and to oversee the care of the poor. The local magistrates are to assist him in their jurisdictions with the tithe and alms, and also with the identification of the very poor and all the information pertaining to them. The poor are to be given not only food and drink but also clothing and everything else they need.

For the proper preservation of general order in the land four captains are to be appointed as well as a commander-in-chief over the whole land who in time of war as peace regularly see to the country's needs. They will be responsible for defence, and the care of the woodlands, passes, roads, bridges, waterways, buildings, and highways; in short, all things the land needs. They will faithfully see that the needs are met. All needs are to be reported to the government after they have been personally examined and

investigated. They are then to act always according to the decision
[18] of the government. Swamps and meadows and other unproduc-
tive areas in the land are to be made arable for the common
good regardless of the possible claims of some self-indulgent
persons. The swamps of Meran and down to Trent are all
to be drained so that many cattle, cows, and sheep may be supported on them, and much more grain may be grown so that
the country will be supplied with meat. In many places olive
trees should be planted and saffron raised. The vines in the vineyards on the valley floor should be trained on trellises [1] to produce fermented red wine as they do in Italy, and alternate them
with grain fields since there is a shortage of grain. The result
would be that the noxious vapours from the swamps would disappear and the land would become healthier. Many illnesses
would disappear which are caused by the heavy wine grown on
the valley floor, wine and grain would be plentiful and could be
raised with minimal expense. The vineyards on the hills which
are not useful for grain should be left for wine production.

In every jurisdiction at locally convenient times the whole
community is to clean up communal fields to provide good pasture and thus to improve the land. No one is to engage in commercial business in order that he may not be contaminated with
the sin of usury. But in order that there be no need, the cause of
good order served, and so that no one will be overcharged and
cheated but rather that honest dealings prevail and good products
be available, one place in the country is to be designated [to centralize the commercial enterprise]. Trent would be the most suit-
[19] able centre because of its commercially favourable location across
the trade route. All industry will be established there such as
the production of silk cloth, hats, brass goods, velvet, shoes and
other requirements. A general manager will be appointed who
will establish prices. Other products which cannot be produced
in Tyrol such as spices would be imported. At several centres in
the land stores will be established according to convenience
where [manufactured products] will be sold at cost. Thus deception and duplicity will be prevented, goods will be available at
their true value, and currency will remain in the land, all for the

---

[1] See G. Franz, *Quellen zur Geschichte des Bauernkrieges*, 1963, footnote 83, p. 288.

great advantage of the common man. The administrator and his aides would receive a fixed salary.

[20] *Coinage*

A stable currency such as that during the time of Sigmund will be established. The present currency will be abolished and all foreign money by which our currency would be measured and valued is no longer valid. Any currency that is comparable in value to our own will be acceptable.

[21]

All the chalices and precious metals are to be taken from every church and house of God and minted into coins to be used for the common benefit.

[22]

Good relations are to be established with neighboring countries. Savoyards are not allowed to sell in the land. One market is to be established in the Etschland and one in the Inn Valley. There will be standard weights, measure, and trade laws. The boundary areas and the passes are to be kept in good order, and a considerable amount of money is to be kept in reserve in case of unexpected war. The property of the exiled nobles and the proceeds of other estates will be used for local administrative costs.

The Mines

First, all smelting houses, mines, ore, silver, copper and whatever pertains to it that is found in the land to belong to the nobility and foreign merchants and companies such as the Fuggers, Hochstetters, Baumgartners, Pimels and their like, are to be expropriated and given over to public ownership. They have rightly forfeited their right to them for they [bought] them with money acquired by unjust usury in order to shed human blood. Thus also they deceived the common man and worker by paying his wages in defective goods, the price of which would have been burdensome even if it had been only half as high. They also raised the price of spices and other products by buying up and hoarding stocks.* They are to blame for the devaluation of the coinage, and the mints have to pay their inflated price for silver. They

[23] have made the poor pay for it, their wages have been lowered in order that the smelters can make some profit after buying the ore. They have raised the prices of all consumer goods after they gained a monopoly, and thus burdened the whole world with

---

* Fürkauf, praemercari.

their unchristian usury. By this they have amassed their princely fortunes. They are now justly punished and their activities prohibited.

The people are to elect a general manager to oversee the whole mining enterprise, who is to render annual account for it. No private person will be permitted to smelt ore. Rather, the whole industry is to be in the hands of the appointed general manager.

[24] He will regulate the purchase of ore most economically. The labourers are to be paid in cash and no longer in wares in order that henceforth the general population and the miners may live together in peace.

The saltworks are to be kept in good order. The land should have considerable income from the mines for it would be best if the government of the land with all its offices and security could be supported by it. If however there were a shortage and not enough income to meet the costs of government, a tax or tithe would need to be levied in order that the whole land bear the burden. Diligence and income from the mines ought to be applied to the extension of the mining industry, for it will in turn provide the most income for the least effort.

This is Gaismair's constitution when he becomes the prince in his chimney corner.[1]

---

[1] This sentence is clearly an addition by the copyist.

APPENDIX TWO

HISTORIOGRAPHICAL REVIEW

The earliest evaluation of Gaismair and the revolt he led appears in the contemporary journal of Georg Kirchmair,[1] who was an official in the New Abbey (*Neustift*) near Brixen when it was plundered by the local peasants on May 12, 1525. Understandably he took a very negative view of Gaismair. He describes him as "a superficial yet cunning man,...a thoroughly bad, evil, rebellious, but cunning man." [2] Many later writers copied him and accepted his judgement, since it already appealed to their own sentiments. Of Kirchmair it could be said, "He was there, and he personally knew Gaismair," which gave his pronouncements an aura of infallibility.

About 1630 Jacob A. von Brandis, then vice-regent (*Landeshauptmann*) of Tyrol, wrote a history of that office.[3] One is astonished to find that he does not mention with a single word the very important Diet (*Landtag*) of 1525, which was called in the midst of the revolt to deal with its demands. It is likely that he regarded it as illegal since the then vice-regent, Leonhard von Völs, was excluded from the deliberations, as was the clerical estate.[4] This Diet together with Gaismair, was to Brandis a loathesome interlude until normalcy returned in 1532 with the suspension of the constitution of 1526. Without doubt this work too influenced Tyrolian historians after its first publication in 1850.

In 1830 Franz A. Sinnacher wrote his monumental history of the diocese of Brixen.[5] His discussion of the events of 1525 in Volume VII shows the revulsion of many nineteenth century Roman Catholic clerics against Gaismair, his vision and his actions. He refers to the articles of Gaismair's famous Constitution (*Landesordnung*) as blasphemy and speaks with disgust of the rebelling peasants. He excuses and

---

[1] Kirchmair, *op. cit.*, 419-534.
[2] *Ibid.*, 472. "Ainen leichten, doch listigen Man ... Ain arg, pöser, aufruerig, aber listiger Mentsch."
[3] J. A. von Brandis, *Die Geschichte der Landeshauptleute von Tirol*, Innsbruck, 1850.
[4] Letter of Johann Kautinger to the Bishop of Brixen of June 19, 1525. TLRA *HR* A IV 30.
[5] F. A. Sinnacher, *op. cit.*

justifies the authorities and their actions, especially of Bishop Sprentz and other officials in Brixen.[6] His work was followed by that of Beda Weber, OSB, in 1849. He includes a discussion of the events of the peasant uprising in his history of the city of Bozen.[7] Gaismair is now described as the chief Lutheran agent in Tyrol, skillfully combining Lutheran antinomianism with social revolt. Weber can barely conceal his admiration for the ability of the man. Nevertheless, Gaismair and the other leaders are depicted as morally reprobate, unprincipled villains who used the occasion of social unrest for the satisfaction of their own lusts.

About the time Weber's work appeared there was an awakening of interest in the history of Tyrol centred at the University of Innsbruck and carried forward by successive generations of graduates,[8] who began systematically to use the vast resources of the Tyrolian archives in Innsbruck and other centres for a reconstruction of the history of Tyrol. Prominent among them were a number of Roman Catholic clergymen whose work was designed to aid the ultramontanist battle against the liberalism which made its appearance in Tyrol about 1840 in the wake of the French Revolution. Thus we get repeated apologetic defence of the Habsburg rulers and administration and the church of the sixteenth century. The new liberalism was seen as an evil reincarnation of the Protestant revolt against the authority of the church, Gaismair being generally seen in the first instance as a Lutheran.

The first of these was Josef Greuter whose lengthy article on the causes and course of the Peasants' Revolt in Tyrol appeared in Innsbruck in 1856.[9] This interesting study bears upon it the marks of conservative revulsion against the revolution of 1848, and it warns repeatedly that the spirit of 1525, epitomized by Michael Gaismair, is still abroad.[10] It is the spirit of anarchy by which Greuter means everything that opposed the church and the order and authority established by the ruling house of Habsburg, incarnate in his day in Franz Joseph I (1848-1916).[11] The calls for social equality made by

---

[6] *Ibid.*, VII, 205, 206, 218, 252.

[7] Weber, *Die Stadt Bozen*, 71-112.

[8] See Otto Stolz, *Geschichte des Landes Tirol*, I. Bd, Innsbruck, 1955, 69-103.

[9] J. Greuter, "Die Ursachen und die Entwicklung des Bauernaufstandes im Jahre 1525 mit vorzüglicher Rücksicht auf Tirol," *7. Programm des k. k. Gymnasiums zu Innsbruck*, Innsbruck, 1856. Oddly enough Stolz in his review of Tyrolian historians (see footnote 8) leaves out Greuter's name, even though his work is in certain respects better than that of the other clerical writers.

[10] *Ibid.*, 36, 37, 39.

[11] *Ibid.*, 37, 39, 60.

the peasants in their submission of June/July 1525 are referred to as "communistic" and the introductory articles of Gaismair's Constitution are said to do the bloodiest Jacobin credit.[12] In this work we also encounter most strongly that traditional total mystical devotion of the Tyrolian to the House of Habsburg. Occasionally His Apostolic Majesty even appears to share the infallibility of the Apostolic Highness in Rome. Ferdinand I is cast in the role of Jesus in the desert winning his victory over the tempter when he thrice rejected the peasant demands for depriving the church of its secular power,[13] and he is then immediately linked in spirit and devotion with his descendent Franz Joseph I, "His truly Apostolic Majesty," and "true son of the light." [14] The study ends with the pledge:

> Auf immer bleibt Tirol als Braut
> Dem Kaiserhause angetraut.[15]

In 1859 Flavian Orgler published a biography of Leonhard von Völs, vice-regent from 1499-1530.[16] While it is based on the sources, anything in those sources which reflects unfavorably on von Völs is simply dismissed as the invention of wicked conspirators.[17] The little journal of Angerer von Angersberg, provost of New Abbey, was published by Theodor H. Mairhofer of the same institution in 1862.[18] The short introduction to the journal shows him to be of one mind with Greuter and Orgler. One should not think, he writes, that the complaints of the peasants in 1525 were really justified. This dissatisfaction was due solely to the work of outside Lutheran agitators.[19] Sebastian Ruf [20] is less negative than the others, but his use of adjec-

---

[12] *Ibid.*, 36.
[13] *Ibid.*, 59.
[14] *Ibid.*, 37.
[15] *Ibid.*, 61.
[16] F. P. Orgler, "Leonhard Colonna Freiherr von Völs, Landeshauptmann an der Etsch und Burggraf zu Tirol 1498-1530," *Gymnasial-programm*, Bozen, 1858/59, Jg. 9.
[17] For example, the grievance submissions of the peasants of Meran, Völs, and Salurn in Wopfner, *Quellen*, 88-94, 152-154, 145-148.
[18] Theodor H. Mairhofer, "Brixen und seine Umgebung in der Reformationsperiode 1520-1525 nach dem ungedruckten Bericht des Augenzeugen Angerer von Angersberg, der Rechte Doctor in Brixen," *12. Programm des k. k. Gymnasiums Brixen*, Brixen, 1862.
[19] *Ibid.*, 1.
[20] S. Ruf, "Geschichte der Bauernunruhen im Unterinntal in den Jahren 1525 und 1526," *Archiv für Geschichte und Altertumskunde für Tirol* III, 1866, 353-368. Hereafter referred to as *AGAT*.

tives indicates his rejection of the grievances and actions of Gaismair
and the peasants as unjustified. Justinian Ladurner, a Franciscan
Superior in Innsbruck, wrote about the events in the southern part
of Tyrol.[21] He too shows marked hostility toward Gaismair and the
peasants.

These men are especially incensed by the antichurch stance of the
rebels and are understandably under the spell of the assertion repeatedly voiced by the peasants that nothing would improve until all
the clerics were killed. Hence they tend to exaggerate the lurid, invent
atrocities, and seem not to have noticed Kirchmair's remark that in
spite of all the material destruction there was very little loss of life.[22]
They all work under the mystique surrounding the role of the Habsburg sovereigns. Those monarchs, they believed, were appointed to
their sacral role by divine providence. Who then could challenge their
right and power?[23]

But there was also a notable exception to this trend. Between 1872
and 1880 Josef Egger, historian and professor at the University of
Innsbruck, published his three-volume history of Tyrol, a major
achievement in historical writing in German at that time, meticulously
and massively documented.[24] He shows genuine understanding of the
aspirations of the peasants, although he is not uncritical of them. He
paints a very dark picture of the condition of the church, especially
the clergy, and of the oppression of the feudal lords, which were
among the chief reasons for the revolt.[25] A tribute to his careful

[21] J. Ladurner, "Beiträge zur Geschichte des grossen Bauernrebells im Jahre
1525. Der Bauernrebell in Nonns— und Sulzberg," *AGAT*, IV, 1867, 85-179.

[22] Kiem, *op. cit.*, 148; Kirchmair, *op. cit.*, 475.

[23] See also Franz Grillparzer, *Ein Bruderzwist in Habsburg* written in the 1830's
or 1840's where these convictions are strongly expressed in opposition to the
democratic surgings in Europe following the French Revolution. Grillparzer was
not Tyrolian but he well expresses the sentiment. Emperor Rudolf II speaks in
Act III:

> Mein Haus wird bleiben, immerdar ich weiss,
> Weil es mit eitler Menschen Klugheit nicht
> Dem Neuen vorgeht oder es hervorruft,
> Nein, weil es einig mit dem Geist des All,
> Durch Klug und scheinbar Unklug, rasch und zögernd,
> Den Gang nachahmt der ewigen Natur,
> Und in dem Mittelpunkt der eignen Schwerkraft
> Der Rückkehr harrt der Geister welche schweifen.

[24] Egger, *op. cit.*

[25] *Ibid.*, II, 76-78.

objectivity may be that he was charged with partisanship by both liberals and conservatives. His work remains important even if it has been superseded at many points by more recent studies.

In 1892 Martin Kiem, another clerical historian, launched a virulent attack upon Egger's work.[26] In rejecting in toto Egger's explanation of the causes of the peasant uprising and the religious renewal movements, particularly Anabaptism, he could himself explain it only as the work of vicious agitators and undisciplined hotheads with the surely unintended inference that the people of Tyrol were so spiritually rootless that they could be led astray by any unscrupulous adventurer. The fact that Egger had already spoken to this criticism in his history [27] did not stop the defensive clergyman from repeating it. His attack seems to have been the deathblow to the extreme clerical conservative interpretation of the Peasants' Revolt, although it once more raises its head in another form in the work of Franz Kolb on Anabaptism, who in a much more irenical mood sees Anabaptism as a case of mental abberation and sickness of soul,[28] brought about by the activities of deluded and fanatical factionaries.

But even the notable secular historians beginning with the year 1900 seem to have worked under the handicap of the Habsburg mystique. For a really open and objective attitude toward Gaismair and the aspirations of the peasants involved some extremely negative judgements about Kaiser Max (Maximilian I) and Ferdinand I (later emperor), who have become almost legendary figures in Tyrolian history. The unshakeable conviction of the unfailing goodwill of the Habsburg *Landesfürst* (sovereign of Tyrol), which deceived even Gaismair for a while, apparently continued to work its magic. The work of Hermann Wopfner, Ferdinand Hirn, and Otto Stolz was based on careful use of available resources. There can be no question as to the excellence and basic reliability of their work. Yet Gaismair is treated as a kind of pariah, and even Stolz, in his definitive history of Tyrol as late as 1955, is careless of details in that he perpetuates the error that Gaismair was assassinated in Switzerland in 1530,[29] when the sources at his disposal clearly state that it happened in Padua in 1532. The more popular history of Tyrol by Alois Lech-

---

[26] Kiem, *op. cit.*
[27] Egger, *op. cit.*, 70-71.
[28] F. Kolb, "Die Wiedertäufer im Wipptal," *Schlern-Schriften* 74, 1951, 45, 56.
[29] Stolz, *op. cit.*

thaler written in 1947 [30] gives the date correctly, as does a doctoral disserattion by Paul von Hoffmann in 1948.[31]

While Gaismair and the peasant uprising got considerable attention in the nineteenth century, it was meant to serve the Catholic church in its battle against liberalism and the preservation of one national faith (*Glaubenseinheit*). A really critical evaluation was therefore for the most part not possible. And while writers like Wopfner and Stolz could forgive Gaismair for heresy they could apparently not forgive him for becoming, in their view, an enemy of Tyrol by going into Venetian service. Gaismair and his movement have received less critical attention by Tyrolian historians than they deserve, especially in view of Egger's judgement about the consequences of the suppression of the uprising:

> The violent suppressions of the peasants' revolt and the religious movement (especially Anabaptism), the numerous executions and emigrations, and the reaction of the lawmakers greatly reduced its [Tyrol's] strength.... They gravely diminished its power and reputation, and in part increased, in part for the first time established its dependence upon the nobility and the clergy. They led to an intellectual tutelage of the whole people by the clergy to a degree hitherto unknown. Its thirst for knowledge was blunted, its sense of freedom stifled, its alertness paralyzed. Along with the French and Turkish wars they led to the financial ruin of the country and changed Tyrol from the most solvent to the poorest of all the crown domains.[32]

This characterizes the peasants' revolt as an event of major significance for Tyrol along with the French and Turkish wars, and with some justification. No Tyrolian study has, up to the present, enlarged on Egger's statement.

Three other Tyrolian historians, Engelbert Auckenthaler,[33] Albert Hollaender,[34] and Karl Schadelbauer [35] have added work on details of Gaismair's life and work and the Peasant Revolt in Tyrol.

The first European writer to offer an extended treatment of Gais-

---

[30] A. Lechthaler, *Geschichte Tirols*, 2. Aufl. Innsbruck-Wien, 1948.

[31] P. von Hoffmann, *op. cit.* Macek's complaints about the bourgeois writing of history are therefore not justified at this point. (*Macek I*, 486, footnote 291).

[32] Egger, *op. cit.*, II, 70. Writer's translation.

[33] Auckenthaler, *op. cit.*, *Der Schlern* 7, 162-167; *Der Schlern* 21, 18-19.

[34] Hollaender, *op. cit.*, 375-383, 425, 429.

[35] K. Schadelbauer, "Die Klageschrift des Deutsch-Ordens-Comthurs über den Bauernüberfall von Vipiteno (Sterzing)," *Der Schlern* 7, 1926, 474-475; "Drei Schreiben über Michael Gaismair im Staatsarchiv zu Zürich," *Tiroler Heimat* N. F. III, 1930, 90-92.

mair was Wilhelm Zimmermann in his work *Geschichte des Grossen Deutschen Bauernkrieges* which first appeared in Germany in 1841-1843. Zimmermann was a Protestant, writing in the heady days of revolutionary fervour and rhetoric after 1830 and preceding 1848. As Abraham Friesen writes, Zimmermann saw history moving relentlessly forward to its goal, a truly free democratic society. Revolutions accelerated this forward movement. The Peasants' War as the first stage in the bourgeois revolution, and the French Revolution with its ensuing revolutions in Germany as its last act, the establishment of a free society.[36]

Zimmermann based himself on the sources; he must have worked in the Innsbruck archives. He did not, however, get a clear picture of the sequence of events and he appears to have used his imagination liberally. But he was the first historian to portray Gaismair sympathetically.[37] His work became the basis for the few comments made about Gaismair by Friedrich Engels in his history of the Peasant War. Although Josef Macek [38] makes no reference to Zimmermann (he does not even include him in the bibliography) he defends the thesis formulated by Zimmermann that the Peasant War was part of the early bourgeois revolution. It was this connexion that motivated Macek to write his great work on Gaismair.

During the period of the Third Reich Gaismair suddenly emerged as a proto-Nazi. Apparently he came to the attention of the Nazi history makers through the nationalistic work on the peasant revolt by W. Zimmermann,[39] and the favourable and fair treatment of Gaismair by Günther Franz in his work *Der Deutsche Bauernkrieg* published in 1933. The accompanying source volume which appeared two years later carried a portrait of Gaismair and quotation from his Constitution on the dust jacket. He was now hailed as the great German revolutionary, held in high estimation especially because of his outstanding military ability. Soon a division of the *Wehrmacht* bore his name, and Joseph Goebbels himself ordered that a film on Gaismair be produced.[40] Work was begun on it but fortunately never

---

[36] Abraham Friesen, *Reformation and Utopia*, Wiesbaden: Franz Steiner Verlag, 1974, 117.

[37] Wilhelm Zimmermann, *Der Grosse Deutsche Bauernkrieg*, n.p.: Verlag das europäische Buch, 1975, 774-797.

[38] See footnote 42.

[39] See W. Zimmermann *Der Grosse Deutsche Bauernkrieg*, n.p.: Verlag das europäische Buch, 1975.

[40] See note 132 Ch. I.

completed. The Tyrolian journalist Anton Bossi-Fedrigotti wrote an essay on Gaismair [41] which began with the sentence, "A Jew was the cause of the peasant war in Tyrol!", referring to Ferdinand's counsellor Gabriel Salamanca. It is a sickeningly tendentious work which deserves to be forgotten for it does both Gaismair and the author deep discredit. This was a most glaring and deliberate misinterpretation of Gaismair and is an example of how an historical figure about whom little is known can be pressed into any mould that men construct.

The first comprehensive work on Gaismair was written not by a Tyrolian but by the Czech historian Josef Macek.[42] It is a work of monumental proportions which deserves high praise for its exhaustive treatment of the subject. It brings together for the first time the vast archival resources in Innsbruck, Vienna, Decin, Trento, and Venice, and corrects a number of misconceptions current until then. His work is very much pro-Gaismair who now turns out to be an early fighter for the classless society. He develops into a man of gigantic proportions, certainly larger than he really was. It is true that he was active in international diplomacy and that he was held in high esteem in Venice and Zürich. It is also true that he was singularly unsuccessful in his diplomatic efforts, not because he was incapable but because no one really took him very seriously as an international figure. Macek gets sentimental when in assessing his integrity he does so far as to refer to Gaismair's "pure heart." Even if we grant that Gaismair's aims and intentions were laudable and his cause just, it remains a fact that he played the same power game as his enemies. He was ready to make weighty compromises to achieve his ends. He too could be cruel and intolerant with those who disagreed with him. But he is bound to show up better than his countrymen have portrayed him because Macek did not hesitate to expose Ferdinand as the double dealer he was for whom the end justified the most devious means. Some will therefore disagree with Macek's interpretation of Gaismair and his work which is representative of recent Marxist historical writing.[43]

But no one can fault his careful assembling of the facts into a powerful and unified piece of historical reporting. He clearly recogniz-

---

[41] Anton Graf Bossi-Fedrigotti, *Tirol bleibt Tirol*, München, 1935.
[42] *Macek I.*
[43] See for example Abraham Friesen, *op. cit.* and Allen Dirrim, *op. cit.*

es some of the major weaknesses and mistakes of Gaismair and the peasants which led to disaster for their enterprise.

Since then, at long last, a native Tyrolian has sought to give Michael Gaismair an honourable place in his country's history.[44] Late in 1970 Hans Benedikter, a journalist-politician from South Tyrol, published his excellent book *Rebell im Land Tirol: Michael Gaismair*.[45] It is written in popular journalistic style but based on source research, and adds to Macek's work at a number of points. Unfortunately for the researcher it lacks detailed documentation, but it is immediately obvious that Benedikter depended heavily on Macek. Here finally the sacral mystique of the church and the House of Habsburg that has inhibited Tyrolian historians for so long has evaporated. This becomes evident in the last paragraph of the book:

> The portrait of the traitor remained. The cloak of silence about Gaismair lies over his homeland Tyrol which he loved, after which he longed in exile, and for whose labouring people he fought his whole life. With respect to this man, who was most likely the politically most important Tyrolian on the European stage, and whose *Landesordnung* belongs to the most significant state-utopias of many centuries, deliberate silence is preserved. The time is past due that Tyrol, and especially Gaismair's own immediate home area, reminds itself of him and gives him the place in its history which is his due. It is time that he receives justice in the name of historical objectivity. Perhaps that would be an important contribution to the unravelling of our complex past.[46]

It is possible that Benedikter's book may be the turning point since it has been very well received, but a major Tyrolian historian has yet to honour Gaismair with his attention.[47]

---

[44] There is one exception to this and that is Holzmann, *op. cit*, who presents a very brief but all in all open and appreciative appraisal of Gaismair the man and his hopes and intentions. See also the drama *Michel Gaissmayr* (pub. Berlin, 1899) by Franz Kranewitter, Tyrolian dramatist. Its premiere excited passionate resistance in Tyrol because he portrayed Gaismair as a man who justifiably revolted against church and authority in his day.

[45] Benedikter, *op. cit.*

[46] *Ibid.*, 253. Writer's translation.

[47] Two reviews of Macek's book have appeared in print, both in South Tyrol. The first is by Franz Huter in *Der Schlern* 42, 1968, 85, and the other in *Dolomiten*, Dec. 4, 1968, a daily paper published in Bolzano. Huter's is little more than an announcement of a new book and not really a critical evaluation. Anselm Sparber, historian from Bressanone, has given an excellent summary of the book. Both are favourable in tone, recognizing that Macek has done a commendable piece of research in closing the gaps in the story of the Peasants' Revolt and Michael Gaismair. Both object to Macek's making a hero out of Gaismair, but beyond

The anniversary years of the Peasant War, 1974-1976, produced extensive scholarly activity on the subject, especially in Europe. Among the public events was an international symposium on the Peasant War and Michael Gaismair, sponsored and financed by the government of Tyrol. It brought together scholars from nine countries for five days to consider Gaismair's role in the total event. While not enough attention was given directly to Gaismair and the revolt in Tyrol, it was nevertheless epoch-making in that Tyrol officially acknowledged the importance of its son Michael Gaismair. The proceedings of the symposium will be published.

This historiographical review is designed to show not only the reason for the silence about Gaismair, but also serves the purpose of identifying the gaps that have existed in the Gaismair story until now. This, so far as the resources were available, has been done in the present study. The Catholic authors were aware of the broad outlines of Gaismair's life and work but their hostility to him and his program made it virtually impossible for them to examine his few writings for purposes of understanding him better.

Macek, in addition to providing the mass of detail about Gaismair's activities also gave some attention to Gaismair's thought, attempting however to secularize this sixteenth century man into something approaching a twentieth century Marxist. Hans Benedikter added little to Macek's story and nothing to Gaismair's thought.

that say not one word about whether Macek's overall assessment of Gaismair is historically justified or not. Sparber even repeats some of the old errors in this summary which Macek has corrected. The major Austrian historical journal, *Mitteilungen des österreichischen Instituts für Geschichtsforschung* has hitherto (March 1971) ignored Macek's work in both Czech and German editions. One cannot help but feel with Benedikter that there has been a conspiracy of silence about Michael Gaismair. Benedikter's book was favourably reviewed in the *Tiroler Tageszeitung* Jan. 23, 1971, as also in *Der Schlern* 45, 1971, 175-176, and numerous daily and weekly papers in Austria and South Tyrol. The reviews were favourable without exception.

BIBLIOGRAPHY

1. PRIMARY SOURCES

The following volumes of copies of official correspondence of the Upper Austrian administration are found in the Tiroler Landesregierungsarchiv in Innsbruck.

An die Fürstliche Durchlaucht vols. I (1523-1525), II (1525-1526).
An die Königliche Majestät III (1527-1529).
An die Römische Königliche Majestät IV (1530-1531), V (1532-1535).
Bekennen (1525).
Buch Tirol I (1523-1527), II (1528-1530), III (1531-1534).
Buch Walgau I (1523-1530), II (1531-1536).
Causa Domini I (1523-1526), II (1527-1529), III (1530-1531), IV (1532-1536).
Embietten und Bevelch 1525, 1526, 1527, 1528.
Gemain Missiven 1528.
Hofregistratur A IV 30 (Miscellanea 105, 106).
Missiven an Hof 1525, 1527.
Oberösterreichische Kammer Raitbuch 1523 (vol. 72).
Parteibuch (1523-1526), (1532-1533).
Tirolische Empörung 1525 Handschrift no. 1874.
Von der Königlichen Majestät I (1523-1526), II (1527-1529), III (1530-1531), IV (1532-1534).

Also the following:

Autogramm E 15.

The following volumes are from the Bibliotheca Tirolensis Ferdinandei (Dipauliana) in Innsbruck:

Codex 1182
Codex 1082

In the Archivio Vescovile Bressanone the following were used:

Bischof Georgen von Österreich Registratur Gemainer Sachen de annis 1527-1530 Codex XI.
Generalraitungen des Stifts Brixen 1525-1527.
Rathsprotokoll de annis 1515-1527.
Registrum notularum Sebastiani Sprenz Episcopi Brixen De Annis 1521-1525 Codex X.

From the Archivio di Stato di Bolzano the following documents:

Cassa 38, Nos. 14 A-F.
Codex 65 Aufruhr und Empörung in Land Tyrol 1525, formerly *Cassa 38* nos. 10B-H.

In the Staatsarchiv Zürich:

Beziehungen zum Ausland: Österreich 1309-1559.

The archives in Munich, especially the Bayerisches Landesarchiv were searched for information about Gaismair, but none was found.

PRIMARY SOURCES IN PRINT

Baumann, Franz L. *Akten zur Geschichte des Deutschen Bauernkrieges aus Ober-Schwaben*, Freiburg, 1877.

Brandis, J. A. von, *Die Geschichte der Landes-Hauptleute von Tirol*, Innsbruck, 1850.

Franz, G. *Der Deutsche Bauernkrieg, Aktenband*, Darmstadt: Wissenschaftliche Buchgesellschaft, 1968.

——. *Quellen zur Geschichte des Bauernkrieges*, Darmstadt, Wissenschaftliche Buchgesellschaft, 1972.

Hollaender, A. "Michael Gaismairs Landesordnung 1526", *Der Schlern* 13, 1932.

Kirchmair, Jörg. "Denkwürdigkeiten", *Fontes rerum austriacarum*, 1855.

Koller, H. "Reformation Kaiser Siegmunds", *Monumenta Germaniae Historica* VI, Bd. Stuttgart, 1964.

Quellen zur Geschichte des Bauernkrieges in Deutschtirol 1525. I. Teil: Quellen zur Vorgeschichte des Bauernkrieges: Beschwerdeartikel aus den Jahren 1519-1525 ed. H. Wopfner, Innsbruck, 1908.

Sanuto, Marino, *I. Diarii* ed. F. Stefano *et al.* Venezia, 1899-1904.

Schadelbauer, K. "Die Klageschrift des Deutsch-Ordens-Comthurs" über den Bauernüberfall von Vipiteno (Sterzing)", *Der Schlern* 7, 1926.

——. "Drei Schreiben über Michael Gaismair im Staatsarchiv zu Zürich", *Tiroler Heimat* N. F. III, 1930.

Tiroler Geschichtsquellen, ed. F. Steinegger u. R. Schober, Innsbruck, 1976.

Frans Schweyger's Chronik der Stadt Hall 1303-1572 ed. D. Schönherr, 1867.

Wieser, E. und Schubring, H. S. *Studien zu dem Film Michel Gaismair* Archivalarbeit Italien-Innsbruck, 1943.

Zwingli, Huldreich. *Sämtliche Werke* ed. E. Egli *et al.* Bd. II, 1908, III, 1914 Leipzig.

3. SECONDARY LITERATURE

Althaus, Paul. *Luthers Haltung im Bauernkrieg*, Darmstadt, 1969.

Auckenthaler, E. "Michael Gaismairs Heimat und Sippe", *Der Schlern* 21, 1947.

——. "Vom Sterzinger Bauernrebell 1525", *Der Schlern* 7, 1926.

Bainton, R. H. *Here I Stand: A Life of Martin Luther*, New York: Abingdon Press, 1950.

Bauer, G. *Anfänge täuferischer Gemeindebildungen in Franken*, Nürnberg: Selbstverlag des Vereins für bayerische Kirchengeschichte, 1966.

Benedikter, Hans, *Rebell im Land Tirol: Michael Gaismair*, Wien, 1970.

Benrath, K. "Wiedertäufer im Venetianischen um die Mitte des 16. Jahrhunderts", *Theologische Studien und Kritiken*, 1885. Heft 1, Gotha.

Blickle, Peter. *Die Revolution von 1525*, München: R. Oldenbourg Verlag, 1975.

Bossert, G. "Beiträge zur Geschichte Tirols in der Reformationszeit", *Jahrbuch der Gesellschaft für die Geschichte des Protestantismus in Oesterreich*, 6, 1884.

Bossi-Fedrigotti, Anton Graf. *Tirol bleibt Tirol*, München, 1935.

Brandi, Karl. *Reformation und Gegenreformation*, München: Bruckmann, 1969.

Brendler, Gerhard. *Das Täuferreich zu Münster 1534/35*, Berlin, 1966.

Bücking, J. "Reformation und Katholische Reform in Tirol", *Der Schlern* 45, 1971.

——. "Der 'Bauernkrieg' in den habsburgischen Ländern als sozialer Systemkonflikt, 1524-1526", *Der Deutsche Bauernkrieg 1524-1526*, hrg. Hans-Ulrich Wehler, Göttingen: Vandenhoeck und Ruprecht, 1975, 168-192.

Dirrim ,Allen. "Recent Marxist Historiography of the German Peasants' Revolt — A critique", *Bulletin of the Library: Foundation for Reformation Research*, Vol. 4, no. 2 (June, 1969).

Egger, J. *Geschichte Tirols von den ältesten Zeiten bis in die Neuzeit*, II. Bd. Innsbruck, 1876.

Engels, Friedrich. *Der Deutsche Bauernkrieg*, Berlin, 1965.
Farner, A. *Die Lehre von Kirche und Staat bei Zwingli*, Tübingen, 1930.
Farner, O. *Huldrych Zwingli*, IV Bde, Zürich, 1943-1960.
Franz, Günther. *Der Deutsche Bauernkrieg*, 1933.
— —. *Der Deutsche Bauernkrieg*, Darmstadt, Wissenschaftliche Buchgesellschaft, 1972.
Friesen, Abraham. "The Marxist Interpretation of the Reformation", unpublished Ph. D. dissertation, Ann Arbor, Mich.: University Microfilms, 1967.
Goetze, A. "Die Zwölf Artikel der Bauern 1585", *Historische Vierteljahrsschrift* V, 1902.
Greuter, Josef. "Die Ursachen und die Entwicklung des Bauernaufstandes im Jahre 1525 mit vorzüglicher Rücksicht auf Tirol", *7. Programm des k. k. Gymnasiums zu Innsbruck*, 1856.
Grillparzer, Franz. *Ein Bruderzwist in Habsburg*, Stuttgart: Philipp Reclam, 1964, 48.
Hillerbrand, Hans, J. *The Protestant Reformation*, Harper & Row, 1968.
Hirn, Ferdinand. *Geschichte der Tiroler Landtage von 1518 bis 1525*, Freiburg i. B. 1905.
Hirn, Joseph. *Die Entwickelung der Landes-Hauptmannswürde in Tirol und die Familie Brandis*, Innsbruck, 1892.
— —. *Erzherzog Ferdinand II von Tirol: Geschichte Seiner Regierung und Seiner Länder* I. Bd. Innsbruck, 1885.
Hoffman, Paul von. *Geschichte Tirols von 1523-1526: Der Tiroler Bauernaufstand*, Innsbruck, Typewritten Diss. 1948 University of Innsbruck.
Hollaender, Albert. "Zu den Bauernunruhen im Gebiete des Bistums Bressanone 1561 bis 1564 (Brixen)", *Der Schlern* 12, 1931, 384-397.
Holzmann, Hermann. "Söhne der Heimat", *Schlern-Schriften* Bd. 232, 1965, 462-464.
Huter, Franz. "Die Bozener Messen", *Illustrierter Hauskalender* 1969, Bozen.
— —. "Macek,¦ Josef: Der Tiroler Bauernkrieg und Michael Gaismair", Book review in *Der Schlern* 42, 1968.
Kaczerowsky, Klaus. *Flugschriften des Bauernkrieges*, Hamburg: Rowohlt, 1970.
Kern, Theodor von. "Zur Geschichte der Volksbewegung in Tirol 1525", *AGAT II*, 1865, 92-95.
Kiem, Martin. "Zeitgemässe Besprechung geschichtlicher Ereignisse. Die Glaubensspaltung im 16. Jahrhundert in Tirol". *Tirolensien III*. Separatabdrücke aus Artikeln des *Tiroler Volksblatt* 90/91, Bozen, 1892.
Klaassen, W. "The Nature of the Anabaptist Protest", *MQR*, XLV (Oct. 1971), 891-311.
Kolb, F. "Die Wiedertäufer im Wipptal", *Schlern-Schriften* 74, 1951.
Kranewitter, Franz. *Michael Gaissmayr*, Berlin, 1899.
Ladurner, Justinian. "Beiträge zur Geschichte des grossen Bauernrebells im Jahre 1525. Der Bauernrebell in Nonns — und Solzberg", *AGAT IV*, 1867, 85-179.
— —. "Die Landeshauptleute von Tirol", *AGAT II*, 1865, 1-40.
Laube, A., M. Steinmetz, G. Vogler, *Illustrierte Geschichte der deutschen frühbürgerlichen Revolution*, Berlin: Dietz Verlag, 1974, 286-290.
Lechthaler, Alois. *Geschichte Tirols* 2. Ed. Innsbruck-Wien, 1948.
Lortz, J. *Die Reformation in Deutschland*, Vol. X, Herder, 1962.
Macek, Josef, *Der Tiroler Bauernkrieg und Michael Gaismair*, Berlin, 1965.
— —. "Zu den Anfängen des Tiroler Bauernkrieges. Der Landtag der Bauern in Meran und die Meraner Artikel", *Historica I*, Prague, 1960, 184-200.
— —. "Das revolutionäre Programm des deutschen Bauernkriegs von 1526", *Historica II*, 1961, 111-144.

Mairhofer, Theodor H. "Brixen und seine Umgebung in der Reformationsperiode
    1520-1525 nach dem ungedruckten Bericht des Augenzeugen Angerer von
    Angersberg, der Rechte Doctor in Brixen", *12. Programm des k. k. Gym-
    nasiums Brixen*, Brixen, 1862.
Mecenseffy, Grete. *Geschichte des Protestantismus in Österreich*, Graz-Köln, 1956.
Mennonitisches Lexikon, ed. C. Hege and C. Neff, Frankfurt a. M. and Weierhof
    1913-1917. 4 vols.
Meyer, C. "Zur Geschichte der Wiedertäufer in Oberschwaben", *Zeitschrift des
    historischen Vereins für Schwaben und Neuberg I*, 1874.
Moeller, Bernd. "Piety in Germany Around 1500", *The Reformation in Medieval
    Perspective*, ed. Steven E. Ozment, Chicago: Quadrangle Books, 1971.
Olin, J. G. *et al. Luther, Erasmus and the Reformation*, New York: Fordham
    University Press, 1969.
Orgler, F. "Leonhard Colonna Freiherr von Völs, Landeshauptmann an der Etsch
    und Burggraf zu Tirol 1498-1530", *Gymnasialprogramm Bozen*, 1858-59, vol. 9.
Reformation and Authority: The Meaning of the Peasants' Revolt, ed. K. O. Sessions,
    Lexington, Mass.: D. C. Heath & Co., 1968.
Ruf, S. "Dr. Jakob Strauss und Dr. Urban Regius", *AGAT II*, 1858.
— —. "Geschichte der Bauernunruhen im Unterinntal in den Jahren 1525 und
    1526", *AGAT III*, 1866.
Schapiro, J. S. *Social Reform and the Reformation*, New York: AMS Press, 1970.
Seibt, F. *Utopica*, Düsseldorf: Schwann, 1972, 82-89.
Sinnacher, F. A. *Beyträge zur Geschichte der bischöflichen Kirchen Säben und Brixen in
    Tirol*, Vol. VII, 1830.
Sinzinger, K. *Das Täufertum im Pustertal*, Diss. Univ. of Innsbruck, 1950.
Sparber, Anselm. *Kirchengeschichte Tirols*, Innsbruck, 1957.
— —. "Vom Wirken des Kardinals Nikolaus von Cues als Fürstbischof von
    Brixen (1450-1464)", *Veröffentlichungen des Museum Ferdinandeum*, 26/29, 1946-
    1949, 344-379.
— —. "Geschichte des Bauernaufstandes in Tirol von 1525", *Dolomiten*, Dec. 4,
    1964.
Stayer, J. M. *Anabaptists and the Sword*, Lawrence, Kansas: Coronado Press, 1972.
Steinmetz, M. "Die Dritte Etappe der frühbürgerlichen Revolution. Der deutsche
    Bauernkrieg 1524-1526", *Der Bauernkrieg 1524-1526*, hrg. R. Wohlfeil,
    München: Nymphenburger Verlagshandlung, 1975, 84-86.
Stella, Aldo, *Dall' Anabattismo al Socinianesimo nel Cinquecento Veneto*, Padua, 1967.
Stolz, Otto. "Die Bozner Messen", *Südtirol* Oct. 1948, 81-22.
— —. *Geschichte des Landes Tirol* vol. I, Innsbruck, Wien-München, 1955.
— —. "Bauer und Landesfürst in Tirol und Vorarlberg", *Adel und Bauern im
    deutschen Staat des Mittelalters*, Leipzig, 1943, 170-212.
— —. *Rechtsgeschichte des Bauernstandes und der Landwirtschaft in Tirol und Vorarlberg*,
    Bozen, 1949.
Strauss, G. *Manifestations of Discontent in Germany on the Eve of the Reformation*,
    Bloomington/London, Indiana University Press, 1971.
Turberville, A. S. *Medieval Heresy and the Inquisition*, London, 1964.
Vasella, O. "Ulrich Zwingli und Michael Gaismair, der Tiroler Bauernführer",
    Zeitschrift für schweizerische Geschichte XXIV, 1944.
— —. "Bauernkrieg und Reformation in Graubünden 1525/26", *Zeitschrift für
    schweizerische Geschichte XX*, 1940.
Volkmar, Hauser. "Michael Gaismairs utopisches Tirol", *Tiroler Nachrichten 87*,
    April 13, 1963, 14-15.
Waldner, F. "Dr. Jakob Strauss in Hall und seine Predigt vom grünen Donner-
    stag 1522", *Zeitschrift des Ferdinandeums 26*, 1882.
Weber, B. *Tirol und die Reformation*, Innsbruck, 1841.

— —. *Die Stadt Bozen*, 1849.

Wetzer und Weltes Kirchenlexikon, 2 Ed. vol. VI, Freiburg, 1883.

Widmoser, Eduard. "Das Tiroler Täufertum," *Tiroler Heimat* Bd. 16 (1951) u. Bd. 16 (1952).

— —. *Tirol A bis Z*, Tyrolia-Innsbruck, 1970.

Williams, G. A. and Mergal, A. M., eds. *Spiritual and Anabaptist Writers*, Philadelphia: Westminster, 1957.

Wopfner, H. "Der Innsbrucker Landtag vom 12. Juni bis 21. Juli, 1525", *Zeitschrift des Ferdinandeums* 44, 1900, 85-151.

— —. "Bozen im Bauernkriege von 1525", *Der Schlern* 5, 1924, 145-149.

— —. *Die Lage Tirols zu Ausgang des Mittelalters und die Ursachen des Bauernkrieges*, Berlin-Leipzig, 1908.

Yoder, John H. "The Recovery of the Anabaptist Vision", *CONCERN no. 18*, July, 1971.

Zimmermanns Grosser Deutscher Bauernkrieg, ed. Wilhelm Blos, 1923.

Zschäbitz, Gerhard, and Franke, Annelore, ed. *Das Buch der Hundert Kapitel und der Vierzig Statuten des sogenannten Oberrheinischen Revolutionärs*, Berlin, 1967.

INDEX OF PLACES

INDEX OF SUBJECTS

INDEX OF NAMES

Klaassen, Walter, 1926-
    Michael Gaismair : revolutionary and re-
former / by Walter Klaassen. -- Leiden :
Brill, c1978.
    x, 156 p. ; 25 cm. (Studies in medieval
and Reformation thought ; v. 23)
    Includes bibliography and indexes.
    1. Gaismair, Michael, 1490 (ca.)-1532.
2. Peasant uprisings--Austria--Tyrol. 3.
Revolutionists--Austria--Tyrol--Biography.
4. Tyrol--History. I. Series.